PROOF

GOD

is

REAL

DR. DANIEL KING

ENDORSEMENTS

This book is essential at helping answer three of life's most important questions. I have known Dr. Daniel King for over 20 years, and he has lived out the PROOF of this book that he shares on these pages. If you've ever had a doubt about God or His existence. This book is for you. If you need help explaining what you believe. This book is for you. Don't just take my word for it. Read it and see the PROOF!
— *Caleb Wehrli* - *Executive Director, Empowered21 - Founder of Inspire International - Tulsa, Oklahoma*

We all have a worldview that informs how we see, experience, and make sense of life. In *Proof God is Real,* my friend Daniel King has provided us a clear, well-researched way to help all of us answer the three greatest questions of life: Is God there? Does God care? And do I dare? (to choose to follow Him). How we answer these questions shapes us in countless ways, now and for eternity. Whether you're a skeptic struggling to understand whether God can possibly exist or a believer looking for ways to better share the hope you've found in Jesus, this book is for you!
— *Kevin Palau* - *President and CEO of Luis Palau Ministries - Portland, Oregon*

In Daniel King's latest book, *Proof God is Real,* he sets out to tackle several age-old questions like: Is there a God? - If there is a God, does He care about me? and, if there is a God who cares about me, what is my response to Him? As Daniel lays out his evidence for God, case for His caring, and hope for everyone to respond to Him he does so with insightful proofs from everyday life, common sense analogies, and well documented facts. Only then does he move to complex evidences and solid Biblical examples. This is a phenomenal read that you will find yourself wanting to underline, highlight, or make a note so you can remember these truths forever.
— *Keith Cook Sr.* - *On the Go Ministries - Nashville, Tennessee*

"We've all had questions about life, God and truth at some point in our lives. In his most recent book, Dr. King presents classical truth in a timely fashion. The threefold division of this book makes it easy and logical to follow the arguments set out. This book is both academically credible and easy to read and understand. You would be remiss not to have a copy on your shelf and one to give away!
— *Dr. Desmond Henry* - *Director, Global Network of Evangelists - South Africa*

Atheism is increasingly becoming a problem, especially among young people. Through so-called "higher learning," people think they have outsmarted the obvious truth that God exists. God does not call atheists intelligent, but calls them a "fool." Atheists don't want to believe in God because belief in God logically leads to accountability to God, and that is the real motive behind atheism. They don't want to be accountable to God. Daniel King does a superb job countering the attacks against God's existence. I fully endorse his book *Proof God is Real.*

— **Tom Brown** - *Word of Life Church - www.tbm.org - www.charismatic.org*

There are three reasons that I recommend Daniel King's book, *Proof God Is Real.* First, although there are several excellent books on Apologetics, this book exhibits these unique aspects: Dr. King's passion for Christ and the empowerment of the Holy Spirit can be seen throughout his entire book. His words have the ring of a heart alive with the presence of God. Second, you sense that this book is not written as a treatise concerning a relevant topic like apologetics but more than that. Daniel's passion to reach men and women comes from one of the leading mass evangelists in the world. This unique perspective creates a manuscript that goes beyond the "if the person asks this question, then say this" approach. Daniel clearly understands that apologetics clears the misconceptions about God and Christ while dealing with the questions caused by doubts. Third, *Proof God is Real* is written by a Christian leader who regularly relates to atheists, agnostics, non-believer's, and believers dealing with doubts. His words are not shared in a ministry vacuum, but shaped by the heart of an evangelist who ably explains that Christianity is a factual faith. I encourage you to read and study this material so you can be "ready to give an answer for the hope that is in you" (1 Peter 3:15). You will be tremendously encouraged in your faith in Christ.

— **Dr. Jim Burkett** - *Director, Apologetics-on-Fire Conferences and The Oklahoma School of Apologetics & Practical Theology*

I want to enthusiastically recommend this book by Dr. Daniel King. The book itself is a presentation of the Gospel at the highest level, disproving most of the excuses people have for not accepting Christ. In your reading you will also find arguments that will not only support your faith, but also provide very concrete and irrefutable evidence about the Resurrection of Christ. God revealed Himself to Dr. Daniel King with this masterful book. I sincerely hope that it be greatly used and disseminated to make many know God.

— **Jorge Ovando** - *IBEM Church - Argentina, South America*

www.KingMinistries.com

ISBN 978-1-931810-33-3

Published by: King Ministries International
TULSA, OK

King Ministries International
PO Box 701113
Tulsa, OK 74170-1113 USA
Product Hotline: 1-877-431-4276

King Ministries Canada
PO Box 3401
Morinville, Alberta T8R 1S3 Canada

www.KingMinistries.com

CONTENTS

Dedicated to the following friends
who helped us publish this book:

James Dutra, Zane & Rachel Bousum, Billy & Marianne Allen, Nijel Rawlins, Manuel & Donna Macias, Joshua & Diane Krishna, Wayne Wakefield, Rhonda Olson, Peter & Janice Hofstra, Richard Benjamin, Pete & Sue Burch, Shelly Billingsley, Dr. & Mrs. Edwell Nhira, Steven & Patti Bickel, Bill & Janet Volkmer, Michael Butler, James & Karen Hosack, Michael & Simone Puccinelli, Ron & Jill Stafford, Mac Barnes, Ricky & Eloise Triplett, Kelvin & Ginger Morgan, Mr. & Mrs. John Chapman, Robert & Susan King, Lauren Clark, Brian & Christa Hart, Rev. Josue Yrion, Brad & Mary Sullivan, Drs. Phillip & Brenda Goudeaux, Elsie Adams, Gordon & Andrea Roskamp, Chas & Joni Stevenson, Jimmy & Mary Urias, Rollan & Barbara Fisher, Tom & Sonia Brown, Patrick Savage, Asaad & Lois Faraj, John & Shirley Tasch, Samuel Yen, Bethany Spaulding, Brenda Judkins, Mason & Emily Crumpler, David & Cheri Harris, Jon & Esther Bucher, Greg Fraser and The Father's House Church, Richard & Joanie Himschoot, Ray & Margo Kirkpatrick, Johan & Jolene Kruithof, Aaron & Cindy Matson, Dorene Pearse, Ernie Pinette, Kenneth Shen, Alisa Shen, Angela Shen, Vision 2020, Nathan & Jessica Himschoot

Special thanks to our friends who helped with
editing, proofreading, and design:

Luke Inberg, May Ling Shen, South River Design, Bryan Citrin

FOREWORD

The Bible says we are to *"always be prepared to give an answer to everyone who asks you to give the reason for the hope that you have, but do this with gentleness and respect"* (1 Peter 3:15, NIV). This is exactly what Daniel King has done by writing *Proof God is Real.*

Dr. King writes with warmth, breadth, and courtesy. Rather than side-stepping objections to faith, he addresses many of the toughest issues with well-informed arguments and candor. Yet he is never combative. Every assertion he makes is embedded in his concern for the reader's spiritual wellbeing.

The author follows in the train of evangelists who were also able apologists, beginning with the Apostles. Peter affirmed, *"For we have not followed cleverly devised myths when we made known to you the power and coming of our Lord Jesus Christ, but we were eyewitnesses of His majesty"* (2 Peter 1:16, MEV). Daniel King, as well, has been an eyewitness to the power of the living Christ in his fruitful, largescale gospel meetings around the world. Much of Paul's ministry was as a church-planting evangelist, verifying the gospel with healings and miracles. Yet every Sabbath, Paul shifted gears and led as an apologist. His habit was to go to the synagogue and persuade both Jews and Greeks of the veracity of the gospel (Acts 18:4). In the same way, international evangelist

Daniel King also has produced a landmark defense for the truth claims of Christianity.

This is, of course, a book on apologetics. Although I have a collection of several such books, *Proof God is Real* is moving to the top of my list to give to those seriously looking at Christianity. As assaults on the gospel of Jesus Christ intensify, the need for this book is indeed urgent. It is a book espousing a particular worldview. Dr. King's perspective on history, the present, and the future is informed thoroughly by the Scriptures. It is a book of theology, for the subject is theology proper (the study of the being and attributes of God). And it is a book on evangelism. The author's heart to see people truly know the one true God pulsates from every page.

As Jim Burkett notes, "Apologetics clears the way for evangelism. It removes the intellectual obstacles and identifies the false concepts that have prevented a person from understanding Christ and the gospel. Apologetics leads a person to the reasonableness of Christianity and to the place where he can hear the gospel of Christ and make a choice."[1] *Proof God is Real* accomplishes this with clarity and cogency.

Non-Christians, including atheists and agnostics, will come away from this book better informed on the crucial issues of belief and non-belief. Christians will see in this book a potent new tool for sharing their faith. A strong part of our stewardship as those entrusted with the gospel is to protect its truth. When anyone messed with the gospel Paul sprang into action. Through this book, Dr. King could echo Paul's defense of the gospel: *"We did not give in to them for a moment, so that the truth of God might be preserved for you"* (Galatians 2:5, NIV). No longer can apologetics be viewed as an "elective;" it is part of the core curriculum for every twenty-first century Christian.

As I read this book, my immediate thought was to get it into the hands of family, friends, pastors, co-workers, and honest seekers. The contents of this book are so rich, so helpful, it is surely destined to become a classic. How Dr. King packed such a treasure trove of insights and information into less than 200 pages is truly amazing.

The brilliant apologist and theologian, John Stott, wrote: "I pray earnestly that God will raise up today a new generation of Christian apologists or Christian communicators, who will combine an absolute loyalty to the biblical gospel and an unwavering confidence in the power of the Spirit with a deep and sensitive understanding of the contemporary alternatives to the gospel, who will relate the one to the other with freshness, pungency, authority and relevance; and who will use their minds to reach other minds for Christ."[2]

Dr. Stott's prayer has been answered. The Lord has raised up, among others, Daniel King. And Daniel King has written a defense of the Christian faith "with freshness, pungency, authority, and relevance."

David Shibley
Founder / World Representative
Global Advance

PROOF

INTRODUCTION

Without faith it is impossible to please God, because anyone who comes to Him must believe that He exists and that He rewards those who earnestly seek Him. — Hebrews 11:6

Have you ever asked yourself, "What is the meaning of life?" Or, "What should I accomplish with my life?" Or perhaps you have asked, "What should I study in school?" or "Who should I marry?" Or perhaps you have gone through personal trauma or a heartrending experience, like a death of a loved one or dear friend, and you have cried out, "Why did this tragedy happen?" All of these are important questions, but there are three questions that are even more important for you to ask.

The three most important questions in life

In fact, I propose that there are three questions so vital that the way you answer them will shape how you answer all the other important questions you ask in life. Your answers to these questions will determine your worldview and life philosophy. They will help you decide what is most important to you; they will influence how you live your life every day; your eternal destiny depends on how you answer them. So, what are the three questions that are so important? Consider the following:

1. Is there a God?
2. If there is a God, does He care about me?
3. If there is a God who cares about me, what is my response to Him?

In the following pages, I will pose these three questions and explain how I answer them for myself. My answers to these questions are based on various proofs, and it is these proofs that I offer for your consideration. While you may not agree with how I answer these questions, the important thing is that you answer these questions for yourself. I do not ask you to answer these questions in a vacuum. Indeed, to questions so important, you would be foolish to trust any answer without examining the evidence.

So, how do I answer these questions? Before I share the answers with you, it's necessary to understand the concept of worldview.

Let's talk about "worldview"

Every person on the planet develops a worldview. A worldview is a belief system, paradigm, set of presuppositions, or philosophy of life that anyone holds about themselves and their world. According to the Christian author, Ravi Zacharias, a worldview should satisfy a person's questions about origin, meaning, morality, and destiny.[1] Every paradigm that is clearly communicated on a broad enough platform eventually becomes part of "common knowledge." People pick and choose from this stock of common knowledge as they develop their individual worldviews. This is why some people are liberals, others are conservatives; some are Christians, others are atheists; some choose to follow Mohammad, others follow the teachings of Buddha; some are vegetarians, others eat meat. And I could go on.

You can think of a worldview as a pair of colored sunglasses. Blue tinted sunglasses make the world look blue and green sunglasses make the world look green. As people experience more of life and are exposed to different ideas, they change the tint of their sunglasses— where the world was blue before, now it seems red or green or golden.

As a result, a person can go through several paradigms as they go through life.

The truth is that no one's paradigm is completely accurate or consistent—some of their presuppositions may be true, partially true, or even entirely false. The Apostle Paul wrote, *"For now we see through a glass, darkly; but then face to face: now I know in part; but then shall I know even as also I am known"* (1 Corinthians 13:12). Simply put, a person's worldview (the sunglasses they are looking through) determines what they see and believe about the world and their place in it. My worldview is a Christian one, and the following pages, as they answer the three questions posed earlier, will help you see what I am seeing through my pair of Christian sunglasses.

A word to Christians

This book falls under the topic of Christian apologetics. The word apologetics comes from the Greek word *apologia*, meaning "to give a reasoned response," and it is used seven times in the New Testament (Acts 22:1, 25:16; 1 Corinthians 9:3; Philippians 1:7,16; 2 Timothy 4:16; 1 Peter 3:15). This word does not mean, "to make an apology," as the modern reader might think, rather, it means "to give a defense." The purpose of Christian apologetics is to rationally examine the beliefs of Christianity in order to give a reason for the hope that is in us (1 Peter 3:15). Apologists defend the faith and combat unbelief.

It is Biblical to use reason to encourage ourselves in our own faith and to persuade other people concerning the truth of God's Word. The prophet Isaiah wrote, *"Come now, and let us reason together…"* (Isaiah 1:18). The Apostle Paul *"went into the synagogue and spoke boldly for three months, reasoning and persuading concerning the things of the kingdom of God"* (Acts 19:8). Believers are called to love God with all their hearts, minds, souls, and bodies (Luke 10:27). In a sense, apologetics is how we love God with our minds.

Since it provides a logical foundation for the Christian faith, apologetics is part of a strong theology. Before we can explain sin and salvation, atonement and the sacraments, reprobation and redemption, we must be able to discuss and defend God's creation of the universe and the historical fact of Christ's resurrection. If God did not create the universe, then Adam and Eve are mythical people and there is no such thing as "sin." If Jesus did not rise physically from the dead, then there is no salvation and no eternal life with Him after death. So, the material covered in this book should be a primary concern of Christian education.

A word to skeptics and atheists

Even though this book is concerned with apologetics, I do not consider myself a professional apologist. I am an evangelist—that is, someone who is committed to sharing my faith in Christ with as many people as will listen to me. My goal in this book is not to argue with you, because I often find that arguments do not convince people to change their opinions. Instead my hope is that you will take the time to look at and understand my worldview.

The difference between the Christian and the atheist is that each of us has a different paradigm (different tinted sunglasses) through which we interpret life. Once there was a philosophy professor who wrote on the chalkboard the topic of his lecture: "GODISNOWHERE." The atheist students in the class read the phrase as "God is nowhere." But a Christian student raised his hand and said, "Amen! God is now here." In the same way, while I see creation and think of a Creator, the atheist peers through his evolutionary sunglasses and sees random chance. I see a miracle; the atheist witnesses the same event and remains skeptical. It does little good for me to try to argue the atheist into believing the world is golden when he can see clearly that it is red.

In the same way, no matter how many arguments atheists have thrown at me, such as that morality is evolutionary, or that belief in God is simply caused by a gene, it doesn't change what I believe. If the atheist rejects the concept of God, then he is forced to look for another explanation for what he sees. But I don't need another explanation, because I already have one that fits my understanding of the facts perfectly well (i.e. God is the source of morality). In fact, I am absolutely convinced that the Bible provides a better explanation for the facts of life than any other paradigm. If you are an atheist, the point of this book is to offer you the view through my sunglasses and present reasons for why I believe there is a God.

For thousands of years, theologians and philosophers have wrestled with the questions I am presenting. Perhaps I should have titled this book *Some Ideas That Convince Me There Is a God and Why They Should Convince You Too*. But it's not as catchy, even if it might be more honest. Indeed, if there was "smoking-gun" evidence for the existence of God, it would have been hailed long ago and there would be no grounds for doubt or disbelief. So the evidence presented in this book is not without counterarguments. However, while each of these arguments taken individually is refutable in the eyes of some, I propose that all the evidence taken collectively amounts to a body of proof. Like a lawyer trying to convince a jury, I hope that you will be persuaded by what I find persuasive. Persuading you is important to me because I really want you to go to heaven with me so we can experience God together.

Believe me, while you may be an atheist, that doesn't keep God from loving you. God isn't mad at atheists. And I'm not mad at atheists either, even though they sometimes laugh at Christians like me. Most of the atheists I have met would make great Christians. By this I mean that they are "good" people, even if they do not believe in God. I like atheists, I just think they are looking though the wrong tinted glasses.

Back to the three questions

1. Is there a God?
2. If there is a God, does He care about me?
3. If there is a God who cares about me, what is my response to Him?

These are the three most important questions anyone can ever ask. The answers to them will give the basic shape to a person's life and priorities and inform decisions great and small. How have I answered these three questions? One profound verse from the Bible gives me the answer:

> *Without faith it is impossible to please God, because anyone who comes to Him must believe that He exists and that He rewards those who earnestly seek Him* (Hebrews 11:6).

This passage tells me three things about God: that He exists, that He rewards those who seek Him, and that I need to have faith in God. To put it another way, the answers to the three vital questions can be stated as follows:

1. God is THERE. So I believe there is a God. This first answer confirms my observations of nature and myself. Because there is order in the universe, something must have given this universe order. Design requires a designer. Inside me there is a sense of right and wrong. Morality requires a moral law giver. These two reasons, more than any others, convince me there is a God. In the first section of this book, I will unfold seven proofs that convince me that God is there.

2. God does CARE. I know that God cares because life itself is mind-bogglingly wonderful. That I can think and feel and laugh and share life with my wife and my children and other family and friends—experiencing what it means to care for others and be cared for in turn by them—tells me that God must be caring too. But He didn't leave it to me to guess about that. He revealed Himself through the Bible and through Jesus Christ to show me what He is like and how much He cares for me.

The Bible is the starting point of Christian apologetics. But what makes the Bible unique? There are many different religions with many different holy books. To leap from the belief that there is a God to the belief that this God speaks in and through the Bible requires faith. But there are many rational reasons for taking this step of faith. The evidence for the life, death, and resurrection of Jesus sustains my faith that the Bible is true. In the second section of this book, I will present evidence to prove that God cares for every person, including you.

3. I must DARE to put my trust in Him. Since God cares about me, He wants to have a relationship with me. According to the Bible, this relationship with God begins when I make Jesus Christ the Lord of my life. A "sinner" is someone who, left to themselves, doesn't give a thought to God. The sin of humankind is obvious. People lie, cheat, steal, and have hate in their hearts for their fellow humans. G.K Chesterton said, "Original Sin is the only church doctrine that can be empirically verified." Original Sin is what the Bible means when it says, *"All have sinned"* (Romans 3:23). All people are sinners, and *"… the wages of sin is death* (Romans 6:23).

But the Bible also says, *"the gift of God is eternal life in Christ Jesus our Lord"* (Romans 6:23), and that *"Everyone who calls on the name of the Lord will be saved"* (Acts 2:21). The day I cried out to Jesus and chose to trust in Him was the day that my relationship with God began. In the final section of this book, I will explain why we must dare to put our trust in God.

If you are a believer, I hope that your understanding of God and the trust you place in Him expands and becomes all the stronger as you read these pages. May your confidence in what you already believe become even more steadfast.

If you are an atheist, or a skeptic, or someone who hasn't given much thought to these three questions, I hope the view through my glasses challenges your certainty about the assumptions you have put your trust in. The choice to dismiss the evidence as insufficient or to prove it by a personal leap of faith will be yours.

Let's get started.

PART 1:
IS GOD THERE?

Seven Proofs for God's Existence

CHAPTER 1

Cosmological Proof—The Evidence from Cause

Premise A: *Everything that exists must have a cause.*

Premise B: *This cause must be a great causer.*

Premise C: *The only causer great enough would be God.*

Conclusion: *Therefore, God exists.*

Imagine a group of friends. Angela needs a jacket because she is cold. She turns to Luke and asks, "Can I borrow a jacket from you?"

Luke says, "Of course, but I don't have a jacket. Let me borrow one from my friend Dalton." He turns to Dalton and asks to borrow a jacket.

Dalton is willing to lend Luke a jacket, but he does not have one either. So he turns to Matt and asks him if he can borrow a jacket. Matt says, "I don't have one, but I know someone who does." He tries to borrow a jacket from another member of the group. That person tries to borrow a jacket from another person.

This series is made up of "borrowing lenders." If there is an infinite series of borrowing lenders, no one will ever get a jacket. If everyone in the group must borrow a jacket, then no one actually has a jacket. For the circle of borrowing to come to an end, someone must actually own a jacket. In other words, to be able to give the jacket to the friend who needs it, you have to stop the series of lenders with a "first lender" who has a jacket.[1]

In the same way, if one thing causes another thing, and that thing is caused by something else, eventually, one has to come to a "first causer." A first causer is an entity that exists by its very nature: an uncaused causer, a necessary being. We call this being "necessary" because without its existence nothing else would exist. This necessary being or first cause is what we call God.

The Uncaused Cause

To address what seems to be a natural and perennial interest in causation, serious thinkers throughout history have developed the Cosmological Proof. This proof states that everything in the universe has been caused, one cause after another, all the way back to a great Uncaused Cause, called God. Importantly for Christians, this argument is validated by the first verse of the Bible which says, *In the beginning God created the heavens and the earth*" (Genesis 1:1).

The argument also bears similarities to Sir Isaac Newton's Laws of Motion. The First Law states that, "A body at rest stays at rest, unless moved upon by outside forces." The Second Law states, "The change of momentum of a body is proportional to the impulse impressed on the body, and happens along the straight line on which that impulse is impressed." The Third Law states, "To every action there is always an equal and opposite reaction."[2] Newton's Laws of Motion tell us that every movement has a cause.

Consider a pool table. The black eight ball stays at rest on the table until it is hit by another object. No matter how long the ball sits there, it will never fall into the corner pocket unless a chain reaction from player to cue to cue ball knocks the eight ball into the hole. Every movement has a cause. The cause itself is a movement. The movement of the cause has its own cause, and so to a chain of causes. But a chain that hangs on nothing is impossible to conceive. Hence the concept of an Uncaused Cause or an Unmoved Mover.

Aristotle (384-322 BC), was the first to propose the idea of an Unmoved Mover. He did not know of the Christian God, but he did understand that someone must be the cause of the universe. Thomas Aquinas (1224-1274), the greatest Western philosopher of the Medieval Age, thought "the first and more manifest way" to prove God's existence was the proof from motion.[3] His reasoning is as follows:

Premise A:	*Things move.*
Premise B:	*Nothing moves itself, since everything that is moved must be moved by another.*
Premise C:	*If that which causes the motion is itself being moved, then it must be moved by another.*
Premise D:	*This process of movement cannot go on to infinity.*
Conclusion:	*Therefore, there must be a first Unmoved Mover, which people call God.*

When Aquinas talks about motion, he means more than movement from one place to another. Rather, he is referring to change of any kind—whether of life, death, growth, learning, heating, cooling, or any other possibility. All kinds of motion or change or development must have an ultimate unmoving, unchanging, complete cause.

The importance of understanding causation led Aquinas to develop further logical proofs, including another version of the Cosmological Proof:

Premise A:	*Things are caused.*
Premise B:	*Everything that is caused is caused by something else.*
Premise C:	*An infinite regress of causation is impossible.*

Conclusion: *There must be an Uncaused Cause of all that is caused. This Uncaused Cause is God.*

In a third version of the Cosmological Proof, Aquinas argued for a Necessary Being:

Premise A: *Things exist.*

Premise B: *Since out of nothing, nothing comes, there must be a Being who caused things to come into existence.*

Conclusion: *Therefore, this Necessary Being, called God, exists.*

Why is there something rather than nothing?

Once there was a child who asked his father, "Where do apples come from?"

The father explained, "Apples come from a tree."

Without skipping a beat, the budding philosopher said, "And where do trees come from?"

"Trees come from a seed."

"Where do seeds come from?" asked the child.

"Seeds come from apples," said the father.

After thinking for a while, the boy asked, "Where did the first apple come from?"

The father replied, "God created the first apple."

"So, where did God come from?" asked the little boy.

Where God comes from is a question asked not just by little boys. If things are caused, it's natural enough to ask, "What caused the first cause?" To the question of "Where did God come from?" the Christian's answer is, "He didn't come from anywhere. God is just there." When Moses asked God, "Who are you?" God's reply was simply: *"I AM"* (Exodus 3:14). God didn't become, He didn't happen. God is the great "I AM"—the One who simply, necessarily, eternally IS. Jesus claimed the same present tense title when He said, *"Before Abraham was, I AM"* (John 8:58).

Christian philosopher, J.P. Moreland, explains that to ask "Who created God?" is to make a category fallacy. The God that I am arguing for in this chapter is a necessary being. If the cosmological proof is sound, then an Uncreated Creator is a necessary being. I am not arguing for a finite being like a unicorn that could be created. I am arguing for a necessary "first cause." By definition, a necessary first cause cannot not exist, therefore it must exist.

What do atheists say?

Bertrand Russell said, "If everything must have a cause, then God must have a cause." Stephen Hawking wrote, "Does [the universe] need a creator; and, if so, does he have any other effect on the universe? And who created him?" Daniel C. Dennett says, "If God created and designed all these wonderful things, who created God? Supergod? And who created Supergod? Or did God create himself? Was it hard work? Did it take time? Don't ask!" Stephen Hawking and Lenard Mlodinow claim, "Spontaneous creation is the reason there is something rather than nothing, why the Universe exists, why we exist. It is not necessary to invoke God…to set the Universe going." If you ask an atheist, "What caused the universe?" he will likely say, "The Big Bang" If you ask, "What caused the Big Bang?" he might reply, "It just happened." For the atheist, everything ultimately comes from nothing.

Atheists criticize Christians for believing in a "magical being" who created everything, but it is surely more absurd to believe that everything came from nothing. "From nothing, nothing comes," or in Latin, *ex nihilo nihil fit*. Imagine a magician who pulls a rabbit out of a hat. A young child might think the rabbit appears from nowhere, but an adult knows that a rabbit does not just materialize from thin air. But this is exactly what the atheist is asking people to believe about the existence of the universe. The atheist is proposing that the universe popped into existence by magic. But not just any kind of magic—this is magic without a magician.

The Creator-creation narrative of Christians and the Big Bang of atheists have this in common: both require faith to be believed. It requires faith to believe that everything came from nothing, that order came from chaos, that life appeared from non-living matter (abiogenesis), and that consciousness appeared from non-consciousness. It is this problem that physicist and atheist, Lawrence Krauss, tried to reconcile in his book, *A Universe from Nothing*. To the question of "How did something come from nothing?" he answers by redefining the word "nothing" to mean "something." He does not know exactly what that nothing-something is, but he hopes that someday science might figure it out. Ironically, Krauss should have titled his book, *A Universe from Something*.

When it comes to answering the question of why there is something rather than nothing, there are only two options:

1. Everything exists because of some inexplicable accident.
2. Everything exists because a Creator caused it to exist.

The evolutionist says that from absolutely nothing, prompted by nothing, and for no particular purpose or reason everything came into existence. As atheist and scientist Carl Sagan wrote, "The Cosmos is all that is or ever was or ever will be." The Christian, putting faith in the claims of the Bible, and supported by the rational argument from causation, knows that there is an eternal Creator who created everything for a specific purpose. *"God said, 'Let there be...and there was"* (Genesis 1:3-31).

A modified version of the Cosmological Proof

The classic formula for the Cosmological Proof presented at the beginning of this chapter starts with the premise, "Everything that exists has a cause." However, it has been pointed out that if God exists, then God also must have a cause. But, since God has always existed, an alternative argument has been proposed. William Lane Craig calls this the Kalām Cosmological Argument. It goes as follows:

Premise A: *Everything that begins to exist has a cause.*

Premise B: *The universe began to exist.*

Conclusion: *Therefore, the universe has a cause.*

It can be demonstrated scientifically that the universe had a beginning. The Second Law of Thermodynamics states that "Things left to themselves tend towards disorder." In a closed system (like the universe), the total amount of usable energy is decreasing and will eventually run out. Scientifically, this is referred to as entropy. Because of entropy, the universe moves irresistibly towards disorder. Because of entropy, the batteries in my flashlight stop working. Because of entropy, a perpetual motion machine is impossible. Because of entropy, the sun will eventually run out of energy and become a cold, dark ball. The fact that the sun is shining proves that the universe had a beginning. Since the universe moves towards disorder, the fact that there is order in the universe today proves the universe had a beginning. And since the universe had a beginning, it must have had a cause.

That something could be caused by nothing is not an answer that Science accepts in any field of knowledge except in the case of the existence of the universe. If an explosion happens in a science lab, the scientists try to figure out which two chemicals reacted together to cause the explosion. They don't throw their hands up in the air and say, "That explosion was caused by nothing." Such an answer would be unsatisfactory as an explanation for the explosion. Equally as unsatisfactory should be Science's answer to the question of existence. Saying that creation does not need a Creator is an explanation that is unjustified by the evidence of the universe.

Nothing that comes into existence has done so without a cause. A painting needs a painter. A house needs a builder. A watch needs a watchmaker. An egg needs a chicken. The beauty of arguing that God is the Uncaused Cause is that He really is the only satisfactory answer to the question, "Where did it all come from?" When applying the Kalām Cosmological Argument to God, this rationale follows:

Premise A: *Everything that begins to exist has a cause.*

Premise B: *God did not begin to exist.*

Conclusion: *Therefore, God does not have a cause.*

The chain of causation ends with God because He alone has no beginning. But God is larger than simply a Being without beginning. As Craig goes on to propose, "If the universe has a cause, then an uncaused, personal Creator of the universe exists, who, unlike the universe, is beginningless, changeless, immaterial, timeless, spaceless and enormously powerful."[4] All this can be known about God through the nature of the universe that He brought into existence. Consider:

1. The cause of the universe must transcend the universe in the same way that a painter is not part of his painting.
2. The cause of all matter must be immaterial because to create matter one cannot be bound by matter.
3. The cause of all space must be nonphysical or else the cause would be bound by space.
4. The cause of all time must be timeless or else the cause would be limited by time.
5. The cause of energy must be infinitely powerful, or it would not be able to create so much energy.
6. The cause of all meaning must be personal in nature because meaning cannot arise from non-meaning.

These observations from the universe reveal much about God. When I think about the universe and everything in it, when I think about the world I live in and the creatures I share it with—from infinitely complex humans to not-so-simple amoeba—all of it convinces me of this:

God is THERE!

CHAPTER 2

Teleological Proof— The Evidence from Design

Premise A: *What is designed cannot randomly exist.*

Premise B: *The universe and living organisms bear evidence of design.*

Conclusion: *Therefore, a designer of the universe and of life exists. This designer is God.*

A cathedral, a computer, a painting, a symphony, a light bulb…what do all these things have in common? The answer: design. Cathedrals are designed for religious experience. Computers are designed to make calculations. Paintings are designed to please the eye, as symphonies are designed to please the ear. A light bulb is designed to produce artificial light. All this design suggests designers. None of these things self-assemble. A cathedral has an architect and builders. A computer has a technician. Paintings have painters. Symphonies have composers. Light bulbs have inventors.

Consider a watch

As an example of design, consider a Rolex watch. Inside the watch are one hundred and fifteen individual pieces fashioned with meticulous care. To name a few of the parts, there is a crown, a crown stem, a ratchet wheel, a barrel bridge, a mainspring, a minute wheel, an escapement wheel, a balance bridge, a tourbillon, a spacer, a yoke spring, setting levers, setting springs, a clutch, perpetual wheels, barrels and weights. All these delicate parts work perfectly together to make three hands move around a dial divided into 60 parts that count the seconds, minutes, and hours of a day. When I look at such a watch ticking every second in perfect synchronization, I know it exists because of a skilled watchmaker.

The Watchmaker Analogy is the classic proof from design to designer. This argument was proposed in 1802 by William Paley in his book *Natural Theology*. Paley writes:

> *In crossing a heath, suppose I pitched my foot against a stone, and were asked how the stone came to be there, I might possibly answer that, for anything I knew to the contrary, it had lain there forever [...] But suppose that I had found a watch upon the ground, and it should be inquired how the watch happened to be in that place. I should hardly think of the answer which I had before given—that, for anything I knew, the watch might have always been there. Yet why should not this answer serve for the watch as well as for the stone? [...] For this reason, and for no other [that] when we come to inspect the watch, we perceive (what we could not discover in the stone) that its several parts are framed and put together for a purpose [...] This mechanism being observed [...] the inference, we think, is inevitable, that the watch must have had a maker: that there must have existed, at some time, and at some place or other, an artificer or artificers who formed it for the purpose which we find it actually to answer; who comprehended its construction, and designed its use.[1]*

By the same logic, when the balance and beauty of the universe is understood, it becomes apparent that it was made by an intelligent designer. Creation tells me there is a Creator. This is the argument from design, or what is referred to as the Teleological Proof. The word "teleological" comes from the Greek word *telos* that means "end," "completion," or "purpose." The Teleological Proof for God's existence argues that the universe and all life is full of design and purpose.

Consider the universe

If you want to know if God exists, just look up. The existence of the stars points to the existence of a great Creator. In ancient times, people tried to number the stars. With the invention of the telescope, galaxies composed of numerous stars were discovered. In 1900, scientists estimated that there were one hundred thousand galaxies. As telescopes became more powerful, the sheer size of the universe became more evident. Now, using the Hubble Telescope, we can see over fifty billion galaxies from earth. With even the smallest galaxy containing more than ten billion stars, the vastness of the cosmos becomes staggering.[2]

It was from this—"the order of the motion of the stars and all things"—that Plato (427-348 BC) argued for the existence of God."[3] In a surviving fragment of one of his works, Aristotle argued:

> *When the night had darkened the lands and [people] should behold the whole of the sky spangled and adorned with stars; and when they should see the changing lights of the moon as it waxes and wanes, and the risings and settings of all these celestial bodies, their courses fixed and changeless throughout eternity—when they should behold all these things, most certainly they would have judged both that there exist gods and that all these marvelous works are the handiworks of the gods.*[4]

The Roman orator and statesman, Cicero (106-43 BC), wrote, "What could be more clear or obvious when we look up to the sky and contemplate the heavens, than that there is some divinity of superior intelligence?"[5] Abraham Lincoln said, "I never behold them [the heavens filled with stars] that I do not feel I am looking in the face of God. I can see how it might be possible for a man to look down upon the earth and be an atheist, but I cannot conceive how he could look up into the heavens and say there is no God."

More important than the words of Plato, Aristotle, Cicero, or Lincoln, the Psalmist of the Bible wrote that *"The heavens declare the glory of God; and the firmament shows His handiwork. Day unto day utters speech, And night unto night reveals knowledge"* (Psalm 19:1-2). *"When I consider the heavens,"* another Psalm says, and *"the work of Your hands, the moon and the stars, which you have ordained"* (Psalm 8:3), the existence of God is obvious.

The Apostle Paul uses the same argument in Romans 1:20: *"For since the creation of the world [God's] invisible attributes are clearly seen, being understood by the things that are made, even His eternal power and Godhead, so that [people] are without excuse."* In other words, the existence of creation leaves us with no excuse for not believing in a Creator. I like what Ralph Waldo Emerson said, "All I have seen teaches me to trust the Creator for all I have not seen." Like so many before me, when I gaze up to the heavens on a dark night and behold the star-filled skies, I say, "Yes, God is there!"

Consider the earth

The earth is amazingly fitted to sustain human life. There are a narrow range of values in a variety of different categories that permit life to exist on planet earth. The probability that these perfect conditions appeared by chance is astronomical. For that reason, the finely tuned nature and situation of the earth is evidence of design.

Premise A:	*The fine-tuning of the earth for the existence of all life is due to either chance, necessity or design.*
Premise B:	*The fine-tuning of the earth is not due to chance or necessity.*
Premise C:	*Therefore, the fine-tuning of the earth is due to design.*
Premise D:	*If there is design, there must be a designer.*
Conclusion:	*Therefore, a designer exists. This designer is God.*

Scientists have discovered more than seventy-five different finely tuned details in our world that are each essential for life to exist. If even one of these conditions was slightly "out of tune," life on the planet would be rendered impossible. Mathematicians have calculated the probability of all seventy-five of these details happening perfectly by chance is less than 1 in a hundred thousand trillion trillion trillion trillion trillion trillion. Here are some of those conditions that make life possible:

1. The distance between earth and the sun. This planet is set at precisely the right distance from the sun. If the earth were a million miles closer to the sun, we would all burn up. If the earth were a million miles further away from the sun, we would all freeze.

2. The composition of the atmosphere—oxygen. The atmosphere is 21% oxygen. If oxygen were 25% of the atmosphere, fires would spontaneously combust. If oxygen were only 15%, humans would suffocate.[6]

3. The composition of the atmosphere—carbon dioxide. If there was more carbon dioxide in the atmosphere, the greenhouse effect would quickly overrun humans and there would not be enough oxygen to breath. If there was less carbon dioxide, plants would not be able to handle photosynthesis.

4. Gravity. The gravitational force acting on the earth is so finely tuned that if it was changed by 1 part in 10^{40} (10 followed by forty zeros), the sun would run out of fuel and be unable to sustain life and the moon would either crash into the earth or escape into space.[7]

5. Centrifugal force of our Solar system. If the centrifugal force of the solar system did not exactly match the gravitational pull of the sun, no planets would be able to maintain their orbits.[8]

6. The placement of the Solar system in our galaxy. If our solar system were farther from the middle of the galaxy, solid planets would not be able to form. If we were closer to the center of the galaxy, stellar density would make our orbit impossible.

7. The situation and size of Jupiter. The planet Jupiter is in the perfect orbit to act as a gravitational field that protects earth from asteroids and comets.[9]

8. The size of the moon and its distance from earth. If the moon were larger or closer to the earth, tides would be much stronger and would wash away our coast lines. If the moon were smaller, or farther away, the plants along the coastline would be unable to survive the lack of nutrient movement.

9. The surface gravity of the earth. If the surface gravity of the earth were stronger, too much ammonia and methane would be retained. If the earth's gravity were weaker, the atmosphere would lose too much water and would soon be unable to sustain life.

10. The thickness of the earth's crust. If the crust were thicker, it would absorb too much oxygen for life to be supported. If the crust were thinner, there would be so much volcanic activity and movement of the tectonic plates that life would be rendered impossible.[10]

11. The precise tilt of the earth's axis. The tilt of the axis is perfect for maintaining earth's temperature and gives us the seasons of the year. If the earth were tilted a few degrees more in either direction, life on earth would become impossible.

12. The rotation of the earth. If it took more than twenty-four hours for the earth to rotate, it would cause huge temperature swings between day and night. If the rotation of the earth were accelerated, it would cause substantial atmospheric wind velocities.[11]

13. The planetary ecosystem. The rain falls, waters the plants, runs down rivers to the ocean, evaporates, and falls again. This water cycle is just one of many cycles including the nitrogen, oxygen, and carbon cycles. There are cycles of summer and winter, and cycles of birth and death. The consistency of these cycles is necessary to make life possible.

14. Proton decay. If a proton decayed any faster, humans would die from radiation. If protons decayed any slower, there would not be enough matter in the universe for life to exist.

15. The polarity of water molecules. If a water molecule had any greater polarity, life could not exist. If a water molecule had less polarity, ice would not float, and it would continue to build up until the whole planet was frozen over.

And that is just fifteen of seventy-five necessary conditions for life to exist. How did such precision come about? There are only two possible explanations: random chance or intentional design. The mathematical probability of life's conditions arising by random chance are so astronomically small as to approach impossibility. So great is the improbability that it takes more faith to believe in random chance than it does to believe in an intelligent Creator.

Atheists respond to the evidence of the finely tuned universe by pointing to the *anthropic principle*. This principle proposes that the appearance of fine-tuning is only an idea that humans have when they can observe their universe. If no humans existed to observe the fine-tuning, the fine-tuning would effectively not exist. Therefore, life exists in the universe, not because of design, but because the universe had the capacity to eventually support life in one of its solar systems (or where multiverse theory is brought in, in one of any possible universes). Richard Dawkins referred to this principle when he wrote, "However improbable the origin of life might be, we know it happened [without God's help] on Earth because we are here."[12]

An early response to the argument of design was written by Voltaire (1694-1778) in his short novel, *Candide*, Leibniz (1646-1716), a contemporary philosopher and mathematician, optimistically argued that the universe was the best possible world that God could have created. In rebuttal, Voltaire penned his satire in which the protagonist air-headedly asserts, "Everything is for the best in the best of all possible worlds." One character, the naive professor, Pangloss, points out that the existence of noses proves there is a creator because noses are perfectly designed to fit glasses. With similar irony, Douglass Adams, author of *The Hitchhiker's Guide to the Galaxy*, mocks the argument from design when he tells the story of a puddle of water that wakes up one day and is pleased to find that his hole is perfectly designed to fit him.

But such responses, rather than dealing with the facts of fine-tuning, simply avoid them. Imagine standing in front of a ten-gun firing squad. The command rings out: "Ready!—Set!—Fire!" All ten guns report, but you are not hit by any bullets. Undoubtedly, you would be surprised to find yourself still alive. Now, if the ten soldiers reloaded and fired again, with the same result—that you were still standing and in good health— you might start to feel that the odds were on your side. If this happened ten times over, surely you would start to ask yourself *why* no bullets were hitting you and how it could be possible that you were still alive.[13]

The truth is that the chances of this world accidentally evolving into a perfect home for the human species is so astronomically small that it would be equivalent to surviving a firing squad of ten thousand rifles, not just once, but over and over again, for many years. In the face of such odds, surely, we have to start wondering *why* this world is so perfectly designed for human life.

Consider DNA

When the kind of fine-tuning that makes earth habitable is seen in living organisms, it is called irreducible complexity. Irreducible complexity refers to the concept that certain biological systems, to exist functionally, must have occurred as complete systems, and could not be the product of successive modifications brought about by natural selection. To go back to the example of a Rolex watch, if one part of the watch is missing, the watch will not work. Charles Darwin (1809-1882) alluded to the problem of irreducible complexity when he wrote, "If it could be demonstrated that any complex organ existed which could not possibly have been formed by numerous, successive modifications, my theory would absolutely break down."[14] Darwin thought the cell was a simple organism, but with modern microscopes the cell is revealed to be a complex machine with many interconnecting parts. Today, human DNA is seen by some as an example of what the father of evolutionary theory believed did not exist.

DNA is the basic building block of life. It forms molecules that contain encoded instructions for the growth and operation of every living organism. DNA forms twenty-three pairs of chromosomes in each molecule that are the blueprint of a unique individual. DNA molecules consist of two strands of nucleotides that coil around each other to form a double helix shape. These nucleotides are composed of one of four bases: guanine (G), adenine (A), thymine (T), or cytosine (C). The sequence of these bases encodes biological information. As the double helix separates and forms a new molecule (DNA replication), it passes its precise programing to a new cell. All in all, the human DNA molecule is composed of over three billion bits of information in a precise sequence. A single cell has more digital information encoded in its DNA then an entire set of Encyclopedia Britannica. Like a Rolex watch, the complexity of DNA is evidence of design.[15]

Richard Dawkins claims there are a "billion billion" planets in the universe. Then he gives the chance of DNA arising from nothing as one in a billion. He concludes that "even with such absurdly long odds, life will still have arisen on a billion planets—of which Earth, of course, is one."[16] In reality, the chances of DNA forming into usable information are vastly lower than one in a billion. In their book, *Answering the New Atheism*, Scott Hahan and Benjamin Wiker write that even for a "small DNA strand of 100 bases—much, much smaller than we find in any actual cell—the odds against getting a particular combination is a staggering 4^{100} [4 to the 100th power] to one against."[17] The difference between Dawkins' information and that of Hahan and Wiker, bears spelling out.

The probability of dealing a perfect hand in bridge, where each of the players receives a complete set of cards, is 2,235,197,406,8 95,366,368,301,599,999 to 1.[18] But the improbability of DNA randomly assembling is much higher—not Dawkins' chance of 1 in 1,000,000,000, but a chance of 1 in 1,600,000,000,000,000,00 0,000,000,000,000,000,000,000,000,000,000,000,000.

The chances of human DNA randomly assembling are as good as the odds that a deck of cards thrown up into the air in the middle of a hurricane will fall to the ground and form a four-story house of cards with each story being a perfect suite of cards in order from high card to low card. With such odds, it is impossible for the precise encoding of DNA information to have happened by chance. When one looks at the complexity of DNA, it is obvious there is a Creator. Intelligent design suggests an intelligent designer. The God of Jeremiah says, *"Before I formed you in the womb I knew you"* (Jeremiah 1:5).

The law of biogenesis tells us that life only comes from preexisting life. Worms come from worms. Mold comes from mold spores. Human children come from human adults. No science lab has ever been able to create life. Science has never been able to get something living from something non-living. No scientist has been able to recreate replicating DNA in a laboratory. The inability of scientists to create life from non-life is not just a "god-of-the-gaps" problem, it is an insurmountable roadblock to the theory of evolution. When I look at my body and all its intricacies, with its millions of cells working together in perfect harmony, I say, "Yes, God is there!"

Consider the human eye

The eye is amazingly complex with many interworking parts. There are three layers of tissue in the eye. The outer layer is called the sclera. This layer gives the eyeball its white color. The middle layer is the choroid. It contains blood vessels that supply oxygen to the retina. The retina is the innermost layer. In the front of the eye is the cornea, a transparent structure that helps to focus incoming light. The iris is a colored ring-shaped membrane found behind the cornea. In the middle of the iris is a circular opening called the pupil that expands and contracts depending on how much light enters the eye. A clear fluid known as the aqueous humor fills the area between the cornea and the iris. Behind the pupil is clear structure called the crystalline lens. This lens is surrounded by ciliary muscles that hold it in place and that also assist in helping us see. To see objects far away, the muscles relax, pulling on the lens and flattening it. To see objects close at hand, the muscles contract, causing the lens to thicken. Inside the eyeball is found a jelly-like tissue called the vitreous humor. After light travels through the lens, it travels through this tissue before hitting the retina. Embedded in the retina are millions of light sensitive cells that are divided into rods and cones. The rods help us see monochrome vision in low light conditions; the cones help us see colors and fine detail. When light hits the rods and cones, the light is converted into an electrical impulse that is carried to the brain through the optic nerve. The brain translates the electric impulse into an image. This cleverly designed and complex process gives us sight.

The eye is far more sophisticated than a camera, yet no one ever thinks that a camera came into existence by chance. But not only does the evolutionary narrative insist that eyes are the result of chance, but it insists still further that this staggeringly complex organ randomly developed not just in one species, but in many species at the same time. The odds are astronomical. The fact that I can see anything at all, makes me say, "Yes, God is there!"

Consider bacterial flagellum

In *Darwin's Black Box*, Michael Behe, a professor of biochemistry at Lehigh University in Pennsylvania, proposed bacterial flagellum as examples of irreducible complexity.[19] The complexity of bacterial flagellum works like a spring-loaded mouse trap. A mouse trap consists of a rectangular board, a trigger, a spring, and a bar. When the mouse moves the bait, the bait jogs the trigger, the trigger releases the spring, and the spring causes the bar to snap down on the mouse's neck. If any one of these pieces are removed from the mouse trap, the entire trap would be rendered useless, and the mouse would run off with the cheese.

In a similar manner, Behe argued, the protein assemblies of a bacterial flagellum are irreducibly complex. The bacterial flagellum is a lash-like appendage that extends from the body of certain bacteria cells. This appendage allows the cell to achieve locomotion. The flagellum consists of multiple parts including the stator, rotor, shaft, bushing, a hook, and a whip. If any one of these parts is removed, the flagellum would no longer work. It is, therefore, impossible for the flagellum to slowly evolve, part by part since no part of the bacterial flagellum could have appeared independently. Such is Behe's argument.

The complexity of so minute a system as bacterial flagellum is truly marvelous. Because of this flagellum, some bacteria cells can achieve amazing speeds in proportion to their size. Some can go as fast as 60 cell lengths per second. In comparison, the fastest land animal, a cheetah can go about 25 body lengths per second. The design of the bacterial flagellum is proof that there is a Designer.

What is simpler: Creation or Evolution?

Premise A: *Something cannot come from nothing.*

Premise B: *There is something.*

Premise C: *These somethings are systematic, complex, and finely tuned.*

Conclusion: *Therefore, there must have been Something capable of designing the complex systems apparent in the universe and biological life. This Something we call God.*

According to the principle called Occam's Razor, the simplest explanation is probably the right one. So, which explanation is simpler?

- The non-living universe appeared from nothing. From this non-living material, life spontaneously arose. This life then mutated billions (if not trillions) of times over millions of years to finally produce…apes. Or,
- A Creator carefully designed and brought the universe, life, and humanity into existence.

Extraordinary circumstances require extraordinary explanations. Minute random changes spread over hundreds of millions of years cannot explain our existence. Science simply cannot explain the origin of life, the origin of biological complexity, or the origin of personal consciousness. If I start with nothing, that nothing will still be nothing whether I wait one year or a million years. The addition of millions of years of time does not solve the fundamental impossibility of design appearing from nothing. Take a piece of iron ore. Lay it on your desk. How many millions of years will you wait before the ore spontaneously forms itself into the intricate springs and levers that enable a watch to accurately tell time? A tiny bird is far more precise and complicated than a 747 airplane. The bird has millions of interlocking cells and processes that work together to keep the bird in flight. It is absurd to imagine that a plane put itself together. But without batting an irreducibly complex eye, the evolutionist says, "Birds appeared over millions of years of evolution."

The evidence from design is increasing. The more we know about the universe and the more we know about the complexity of biological life, the more apparent it is that we and our world have been carefully designed. Only someone intent on denying the existence of a Creator believes that the staggering symmetry of the universe is a random occurrence or that the intricate design of the human body could drag itself up from the primordial mud. From the enormous cosmos to the microscopic cell, one thing is obvious:

God is THERE!

CHAPTER 3

Ontological Proof—The Evidence from Abstract Reasoning

Premise A: *God has all perfection.*
Premise B: *Existence is a perfection.*
Conclusion: *Therefore, God exists.*[1]

Ontology refers to the area of metaphysics that tries to answer the question of what exists. This kind of philosophical discipline relies largely on abstract reasoning to arrive at its conclusions—abstract reasoning meaning that if all you could do was think, how could you prove that something exists? The famous statement by the French philosopher and scientist, Rene Descartes (1596-1650), "I think, therefore I am," is an example of ontological reasoning. Apologists have used ontological reasoning to prove the existence of God.

Anselm and the perfectness of God

Anselm (1033-1109), Archbishop of Canterbury, was the first to articulate the ontological proof for God's existence in his work, *Proslogion: Faith in Search of Understanding.* The book contains a prayer in which Anselm asks God to reveal an argument for His existence that would be convincing to the atheistic "fool" of Psalm 14:1. That prayer is as follows:

And so, Lord, do you, who do give understanding to faith, give me, so far as you know it to be profitable, to understand that you are as we believe; and that you are that which we believe. And indeed, we believe that you are a being than which nothing greater can be conceived. Or is there no such nature, since the fool has said in his heart, there is no God? (Psalm 14:1). But, at any rate, this very fool, when he hears of this being of which I speak—a being than which nothing greater can be conceived—understands what he hears, and what he understands is in his understanding; although he does not understand it to exist.

For, it is one thing for an object to be in the understanding, and another to understand that the object exists. When a painter first conceives of what he will afterwards perform, he has it in his understanding, but he does not yet understand it to be, because he has not yet performed it. But after he has made the painting, he both has it in his understanding, and he understands that it exists, because he has made it.

Hence, even the fool is convinced that something exists in the understanding, at least, than which nothing greater can be conceived. For, when he hears of this, he understands it. And whatever is understood, exists in the understanding. And assuredly that, than which nothing greater can be conceived, cannot exist in the understanding alone. For, suppose it exists in the understanding alone: then it can be conceived to exist in reality; which is greater.

Therefore, if that, than which nothing greater can be conceived, exists in the understanding alone, the very being, than which nothing greater can be conceived, is one, than which a greater can be conceived. But obviously this is impossible. Hence, there is doubt that there exists a being, than which nothing greater can be conceived, and it exists both in the understanding and in reality.

The prayer proposes that God must exist because He is the greatest being that can be imagined, the being "which nothing greater can be conceived." As Anselm unfolds the ontological argument for God's existence in the chapters that follow the prayer, he proposes that if a being exists in the mind, but not in reality, then a greater being could be imagined who would exist in both the mind and in reality. But God, by definition, is infinitely great; no one can surpass His greatness. The Bible anticipates Anslem's proof in Psalms 95:3, where it reads, *"For the Lord is the great God, and the great King above all gods."* Psalms 145:3 again speaks about the greatness of God: *"Great is the Lord, and greatly to be praised; and His greatness is unsearchable."* Since God is infinitely great, Anselm concludes, He is great in every conceivable way—including in the reality of His existence.

Consider: As humans, we understand the concept of "good." It is "good" for me to have a warm place to lay my head at night. It would be "bad" for me to be outside freezing in the cold. I can also imagine a "greater good" than having an indoor place to sleep. If I am sleeping on a floor, I can imagine the "greater good" of sleeping on a mattress. As I am sleeping in my house, I can imagine the "greater good" of sleeping in a beautiful palace. For each good that I can imagine, I can always imagine still greater and greater degrees of goodness—even if I have never experienced them. For instance, kindness is a form of goodness. If I am a "good" person, then I am kind to those around me. I have been kind on occasion, but I am not as kind as I could be. Nonetheless, I can imagine a being who is perfectly kind. If the concept of "good" is extended in all areas to its farthest possible extent, we come to the concept of "perfection." Anselm argues that if there is a being who is perfect in all ways of being, that being must exist because one of the qualities of perfection is actual existence. This Being who is perfect in all ways of being, including of existence, is the One we call God.

The Christian concept of God is one of a God who is "maximally great." He is like a baseball player who bats a thousand and always hits a homerun. He is like a bowler who bowls a perfect 300 on every game. He is like a contestant who could not lose on a game show. If He were on Jeopardy, He would answer every question exactly. If He were on Wheel of Fortune, He would know the exact weight to give the wheel so He could never lose money, and He would be able to solve all the puzzles without even asking for a letter. The God of the Bible is such a

God. He is perfectly powerful (omnipotent), perfectly knowledgeable (omniscient), perfectly good (omni-benevolent), and perfectly present (omnipresent). He is a perfect being because He possesses to the maximum level all the qualities that are better to have than to not have. And God is maximally great in all areas without slipping over into logical fallacies. In the same way it is impossible to have a "square circle" or a "married bachelor," it is impossible for God to create a rock so big that He cannot move it. To speak of a perfect being, is to speak of God. As existence is a perfection of being, then God must exist.

Does the perfect unicorn exist?

There are critics of the Ontological Proof.[2] Gaunilo of Marmoutiers, one of Anselm's contemporaries, made fun of his argument by proposing an "island that is greater than any other island that can be conceived." Since such an island does not exist, he said that God's existence couldn't be proved by Anslem's kind of reasoning. Similarly, the non-existence of unicorns could be seen to invalidate Anselm's proof. My daughter is eight years old and, like many little girls, she loves unicorns. One day we talked about the perfect unicorn. According to her, the perfect unicorn is pink and has a purple mane and a sparkling white horn. This unicorn would also be magical and sentient. Of course, no matter how perfectly she imagines this perfect pet unicorn, my daughter knows the unicorn will never actually exist. Why can't my daughter's perfectly imagined unicorn or the perfect island of Gaunilo exist, but the perfect God of our thoughts be proven to exist by the very fact that He can be imagined?

Anselm responded to his critics by replying that his proof only applied to concepts with necessary existence. Anselm meant that his argument only works for God's existence because only God's existence is necessary—certainly more necessary than the existence of a magical unicorn or a great island. A maximally great being grounds concepts like kindness and goodness that are part of perfection. A unicorn or island could not be the ground of perfection except by having *all* perfections. The perfect island, to be the perfect island doesn't need all perfections, such as kindness or moral goodness for instance. If it had all perfections, it would no longer be an island, but something else (in fact, God). The ontological proof only works for God because there can only be one maximally great being or entity in existence.

A modern defense of the Ontological Proof

Alvin Plantinga, an American philosopher, has offered a robust modern defense of the Ontological Proof.[3] His argument is as follows:[4]

Premise A: *It is possible that a maximally great being exists.*

Premise B: *If it is possible that a maximally great being exists, then a maximally great being exists in some possible world.*

Premise C: *If a maximally great being exists in some possible world, then it exists in every possible world.*

Conclusion: *If a maximally great being exists in every possible world, then it exists in the actual world.*

In his discussion of the Ontological Argument, Plantinga brings in a hypothesis of modern physics that proposes the existence of multiple or parallel universes. He argues that the existence of God is not logically contradictory and is therefore possible. God being a logical possibility, it is possible that He exists in one of the possible universes proposed by multiple universe theory. Since it is possible for God to exist in one possible universe, then being maximally great, God must also exist in every universe—including ours. As a consolation to my daughter, Plantinga's thinking makes it possible for my daughter's unicorn to exist in some world that multiple universe theory makes possible. But since a unicorn is not a maximally great being, it does not exist in every possible world, and certainly does not exist in the one we can verify.

When I think about God—in all the maximum perfection of His greatness and goodness—just the fact that I can think about Him in this way tells me that:

God is THERE!

PROOF

CHAPTER 4
Morality Proof—The Evidence from Right and Wrong

Premise A: *If God does not exist, objective moral values do not exist.*

Premise B: *Objective moral values do exist.*

Conclusion: *Therefore, God exists.*

Imagine living in a world where there was no right or wrong.

- Someone could kill your loved one, but, because there is no right or wrong, they would not be guilty of injustice. There would be no law by which they could be apprehended or convicted as a murderer.

- You could walk into the nearest jewelry store, smash the glass, and fill your gym bag with as many diamonds and gems as you could manage to get away with. The owner of the store would have no moral reason to stop you from taking what is not yours.

- A husband coming home from a tough day at work could start slapping his wife and abusing his children. But you wouldn't be able to call the police about it, because spousal abuse wouldn't be wrong.

In a world without morality, a terrorist could kill hundreds of people, a modern Hitler could commit a new Holocaust, racism would be okay, misogyny couldn't be condemned, corruption in government couldn't be wrong, and it wouldn't be bad to take away someone's freedom. I don't know about you, but I wouldn't want to live in a world where there is no right and wrong. Thankfully, I don't have to. Right and wrong exist, and the conscience of everyone in the world is proof of this fact.

An objectively moral universe

Have you ever felt you were treated unjustly? Perhaps someone broke a promise they had made to you; perhaps they cheated you in some way or stole from you; perhaps they told a lie about you or broke your trust in another way; perhaps they were violent to you and physically hurt you. How did that make you feel? When such things happen to us, or we see them happen to someone else, we know that those things are wrong and that they should not happen. In the same way that we know what is wrong, we also know what is right. It is right to be kind to people. It is right to be honest and sincere. It is right to be patient and generous. No one needs a law to tell them that patience or generosity or kindness are right. We know that these kinds of actions are right because, when we see people acting this way, or experience it for ourselves, we start to think that the world isn't so bad after all. As the saying goes, "our faith in humanity is restored."

We know right from wrong not just by how it makes us feel when we are treated rightly or wrongly, but also because of what we experience when we treat someone else rightly or wrongly. Inside of every person is a moral compass—the conscience. The word "conscience" comes from joining two words together. The first word, *con*, means "with"; the second word, *science*, means "knowledge." Conscience means that when we do rightly or wrongly, we do it "with knowledge." When we knowingly do what is right, it makes us feel good, but when we knowingly do what is wrong, it makes us feel guilty. The difference between humans and animals is morality. Animals do not have a conscience. Sometimes a mother dog will eat her own puppies with no pain or guilt. A female praying mantis consumes the male after mating with him. A lion does not feel remorse after killing a young zebra. But, if someone treats another human the way animals treat each other, we call that person a criminal.

This knowledge of right and wrong is what the German philosopher, Immanuel Kant (1724-1804), called a "categorical imperative."[1] By "categorical" he means that everyone has a category of understanding that some things are right and other things are wrong; by "imperative" he means that everyone is impelled to act upon this moral understanding. In fact, so strong is this universal moral sense, that even when someone tries to ignore or erase it, the moral sense remains. That is why we feel guilty when we do the things that we know are wrong even if they make us feel good in the moment. That is why we still feel good when we make a right decision, even if it costs us something valuable or makes us give up a pleasure. This sense of right and wrong, of guilt and goodness are experiences that both theist and atheist can agree on. For C.S. Lewis (1898-1963), failing to understand this innate moral sense is like failing to understand the basic laws of the universe:

> These then are the two points that I wanted to make. First, that human beings, all over the earth, have this curious idea that they ought to behave in a certain way, and cannot really get rid of it. Secondly, that they do not in fact behave in that way. They know the Law of Nature; they break it. These two facts are the foundation of all clear thinking about ourselves and the universe we live in.[2]

By the term "Law of Nature," Lewis means that our world is an objectively moral universe. The universe is observed to work in one way and not another—that is what is meant when anyone refers to the "laws" that govern it. These laws do not require us to believe in them for them to be true. Gravity does not exist because we believe in it, nor did it begin to exist when Newton discovered it. Regardless of what anyone believes about gravity, gravity exists and has always existed as a necessary part of the physical universe. Gravity is true everywhere and for all time—this is what makes it universal. Gravity exists independently of what anyone believes about it—this is what makes it objective. The same concepts of universality and objectivity apply to the ideas of right and wrong.

The law of nature, or natural law, refers to what is objectively true about all people as individuals and as societies. "The Laws of Nature and of Nature's God" are the basis of the Constitution of the United States. When it is said that everyone has an innate sense of right and wrong, that means two things. First, because everyone has a moral sense, it is universal. Second, because people are born with this moral sense and have no control over whether they will have it or not, it is objective. In the same way that we don't get to choose if gravity exists, we don't get to choose the existence of right and wrong or if we have a conscience. Simply, we are part of a moral universe where there are objective moral values of right and wrong, good and evil, justice and injustice.

Where does this moral law come from?

Just like the physical universe, the objective moral universe doesn't come from nothing. All people have a conscience and are born with it. That conscience does not come from nothing. The knowledge of right and wrong comes from God. God is good and everything He does is good and just. Even if people have no knowledge of God, God has given people a conscience that tells them what is good and just. As it says in Romans 2:14-25:

> *...for when Gentiles, who do not have the law* [of God—that is the Law of Moses], *by nature do the things in the law, these, although not having the law, are a law to themselves, who show the work of the law written in their hearts, their conscience also bearing witness, and between themselves their thoughts accusing or else excusing them.*

God is the only possible source of an objective right or wrong. Atheists might reply that rules are created by society and that anything society approves of is right and what society disapproves of is wrong.[3] To support their argument they point to examples of how morals can differ from culture to culture depending on the subjective will of the majority. Thus, while most cultures agree that cannibalism is wrong, in some tribes in Papua New Guinea it is considered noble to eat your enemy. But is that the same thing as believing that cannibalism is a moral good? While the cannibal chief may eat people, if we say to him, "Today, we eat your child," he knows that eating his child is wrong. He does not celebrate the announcement as a victory for cannibalism. For thousands of years, cultures around the world have practiced the same moral values we practice today. In every society, some actions are considered good and some are considered bad. Murder, theft, and lying have all been considered wrong throughout human history. If there is a moral law, then there must be a moral lawgiver.

If there is true justice, there must be a just judge to dispense it. This judge must be morally perfect. To make perfect judgments, this judge must be all-knowing. To enforce his judgment, this judge must also be all-powerful. Thus, our innate sense of right and wrong and our inherent desire for justice requires a completely moral lawgiver who is all-knowing and all-powerful. This perfect, omniscient, and omnipotent judge we call God.

Do right and wrong exist without God?

If there is no God, morality is just a random product of evolution and there is no basis upon which to objectively determine right from wrong. Without a supreme moral referee, the words "right" and "wrong" have no objective meaning. The choice between them has exactly the moral significance of a choice between McDonald's and Chick-Fil-A. They simply mean, "I like it" or "I don't like it" or "society likes it" or "society doesn't like it."

Where morals become subjective and relative, no one has real authority to say that anyone else's morals are wrong. In such a godless world, all possible actions become permissible. Indeed, we see that when God is removed from the moral equation, society slips towards the philosophy that, "If it feels right, then it is right." The result is a society that increasingly celebrates uninhibited sexuality, homosexual marriage, and the killing of unborn babies. While godless people celebrate these changes in society, they fail to see that the flat, broad highway of moral relativism gradually leads to the cliff of social disintegration. If morals are relative, how can we say that slavery, or pedophilia, or human trafficking, or racism, or colonialism, or misogyny, or tyranny are wrong? Ultimately, without an external morality the only rule that survives is that "might makes right." Without God, morality and society fall apart—a truth that even the atheist Voltaire understood when he said, "If God did not exist, it would be necessary to invent him."

Often atheists accuse God of being evil, referring to Biblical accounts of when He asked Abraham to sacrifice his son Isaac on an altar (Genesis 22:2) or when He commanded Saul to destroy the Amalekites (1 Samuel 15:1-3). But, the atheist's accusation against the Christian God is built on quicksand since he has no objective foundation on which to build a moral claim. Such an accusation requires the existence of absolute moral values. But to have absolute moral values, there must be an absolute moral lawgiver. The moment an atheist makes a value judgement and says something is good or evil, he becomes evidence for the existence of God.

Euthyphro's Dilemma

The problem of evil is not new. It has bedeviled philosophers for ages. Plato wrote a dialogue about a conversation between Socrates and Euthyphro. In the conversation, Euthyphro, a young man, explains that he wants to charge his father with manslaughter because his father killed a worker who had killed a slave that belonged to the family estate. After a long conversation about the nature of right and wrong, Socrates proposes what is known as "Euthyphro's Dilemma." He says, "I will amend the definition [of good and evil] so far as to say that what all the gods hate is impious, and what they love pious or holy; and what some of them love and others hate is both or neither. Shall this be our definition of piety and impiety?"

Euthyphro replies, "Yes, I should say that what all the gods love is pious and holy, and the opposite which they all hate, impious."

Socrates then says, "The point which I should first wish to understand is whether the pious or holy is beloved by the gods because it is holy, or holy because it is beloved of the gods."

In other words, "Does God command something because it is good, or is something good because God commands it?" The first half of the dilemma proposes that good is a concept to which God subjects Himself; the second half of the dilemma proposes that God can arbitrarily decide what is good. The solution to this dilemma is this: God, being supreme, cannot be subject to goodness, and goodness, to be good, cannot arbitrarily be subject to God. Rather, goodness is both an integral part of God and an independent expression. To understand the resolution of the dilemma, consider the difference between sunlight and the sun. Sunlight is not the sun, but sunlight would not exist except for the sun. At the same time, though the sun is not the light it gives off, yet by sheer force of what it is, it must shine. Even so, because of God, goodness cannot help being; and, God, being, cannot help being good. What God wills and wills us to do is good because He is good. It is God's character that defines what is good, and God cannot do anything out of character. That's what James 1:17 means when it says that *"Every good gift and every perfect gift comes down from the Father of lights with whom there is no variation or shadow of turning."* Like the sun, God doesn't cast a shadow. *"He cannot be tempted by evil,"* James 1:13 says, *"nor does He Himself tempt anyone,"* because (as another verse says), *"in Him is no darkness at all"* (1 John 1:5).

Atheists reject God's moral law because they do not want to be held accountable

Whether accusing God of some inconsistency or denying His existence, the atheist's intellectual problems are often a smoke screen hiding the real issue: the atheist's desire to escape the responsibility that the existence of God involves him in.[4] By denying the existence of God, the atheist is absolved of his sins without incurring the smallest act of penance. After all, if there is no ultimate right and wrong, then there is no personal right and wrong. All is permitted so long as society is not outraged. Without the moral law, hedonism becomes the purpose of existence. But if such is the meaning of the universe, what motivation can there be for me to go to work in the morning, or to love my wife, or even to be alive? If I did not believe that God existed, I know I would behave in immoral ways because I wouldn't be kept from doing them by a moral sensitivity. Many atheists have chosen not to believe in God, not because of intellectual reasons, but because they want to live life free of God's moral laws.

In his novel, *The Brothers Karamazov*, Fyodor Dostoyevsky (1821-1881) points out the reason that atheists reject God. "Without God and immortal life [...] all things are lawful then, they can do what they like."[5] The same character, Dimitri, goes on to say:

> *It's God that's worrying me. That's the only thing that's worrying me. What if he doesn't exist? What if [atheists] are right—that it's an idea made up by men? Then if he doesn't exist, man is the chief of the earth, of the universe. Magnificent! Only how is he going to be good without God? That's the question. I always come back to that. For whom is man going to love then? To whom will he be thankful? To whom will he sing the hymn? [Atheists] laugh. [Atheists] say that one can love humanity without God. Well, only a sniveling idiot can maintain that.[6]*

The truth is that everyone knows there is a God and the people who claim there is no God have suppressed the truth because they want to continue to sin. The Apostle Paul writes of those

> *...who suppress the truth in unrighteousness, because what may be known of God is manifest in them, for God has shown it to them. For since the creation of the world His invisible attributes are clearly seen, being understood by the things that are made, even His eternal power and Godhead, so that they are without excuse.* (Romans 1:18-20)

All creation points to the existence of God. If this was not enough, He also wrote His law on the hearts of every person, giving them the moral compass of the conscience as further proof that He is there. Yet, even with the evidence in front of them and inside of them, people suppress the truth and deny God's existence because they prefer to do what is wrong rather than repent and change. So Paul continues:

> *And even as they did not like to retain God in their knowledge, God gave them over to a debased mind, to do those things which are not fitting; being filled with all unrighteousness, sexual immorality, wickedness, covetousness, maliciousness; full of envy, murder, strife, deceit, evil-mindedness; they are whisperers, backbiters, haters of God, violent, proud, boasters, inventors of evil things, disobedient to parents, undiscerning, untrustworthy, unloving, unforgiving, unmerciful...* (Romans 1:28-31)

It's one thing when we want to hang ourselves, it's a more terrible thing when God hands us the rope. To those who want to sin, God does not hold them back. Ultimately, sin leads to spiritual death: *"...those who practice such things are deserving of death..."* (Romans 1:32). But the good news is that *"the goodness of God leads you to repentance"* (Romans 2:4).

When I think about good and evil, right and wrong, justice and injustice; when my conscience tells me that I fall short of my own moral standard; when I realize that God is good and wants to help me be good, the truth comes home all the stronger:

God is THERE!

CHAPTER 5

Scripture Proof—Evidence from the Bible

Premise A: *The Bible says God exists.*

Premise B: *The Bible is trustworthy.*

Conclusion: *Therefore, God exists.*

When I was a child, I learned a song in Sunday school—perhaps you've heard it:

> *Jesus loves me this I know,*
> *For the Bible tells me so.*

At a very basic level, this simple song expresses the believer's position concerning the Holy Bible. What Christians believe about God, they believe because of the Bible. To a Christian, the Bible is to be believed because it is the Word of God. If the question is asked: How do Christians know that God exists? The answer is: Because the Bible says that God exists.

When hearing such an assertion, an atheist might accuse Christians of circular reasoning, or what is known in philosophy as "begging the question"—which means that the answer is assumed in the question.

But the truth is that every worldview depends upon this kind of reasoning. Every worldview starts with propositions that are assumed to be true and cannot absolutely be proved. For instance, the atheistic viewpoint begins with a presupposition that God does not exist. This is a supposition that cannot be proved to be true. But based on this supposition, atheists argue that the various proofs for the existence of God are wrong because He does not exist.

As atheists have their presuppositions, so too do Christians. Christians choose the Bible as a foundation for belief. Why believe in God? The Bible tells us to. Why believe God is eternal, omniscient, omnipotent, omnipresent, and omni-benevolent? Because all these characteristics of God are clearly stated by the Bible. Why do Christians believe that Jesus is God, and that, as the Son of God, He was born of a virgin, lived a perfect life, died on the cross, and rose from the dead to save humanity from sin? Because, once again, that is what the Bible says. Why believe the Bible is the Word of God? Because the Bible says it is the Word of God.

General Revelation and Special Revelation

The term revelation refers to "knowledge about God." Historically, theologians have distinguished between two different types of revelation, general revelation and special revelation. General revelation or natural revelation refers to what can be known about God from nature through reason. The two avenues of general revelation are creation and conscience. The Apostle Paul talks about these two avenues when he writes of how all of creation points toward God (Romans 1:18-20) and of the law of right and wrong that is written on the heart of each person (Romans 2:14-16). These two avenues have been covered in the preceding chapters.

Special revelation or supernatural revelation refers to what is known about God by divine intervention—such as through dreams, visions, theophanies, or a specific word from God. To discuss these two kinds of revelation, Thomas Aquinas divided truth into two categories: the realm of nature and the realm of grace. What the realm of nature could not teach, the realm of grace could reveal. It was through the realm of grace that God as the Trinity of Father, Son, and Holy Spirit were revealed—a thing impossible to know simply through observation of the natural world or from logical deductions. John Calvin (1509-1564) essentially agreed with Aquinas, allowing that, while it is possible to know God from creation, what can be known by that means is limited. Only a special revelation through grace would enable people to have a clearer vision of God. Karl Barth (1886-1968) believed that the only way to know about God was through the most special, most supernatural revelation of all: the incarnation of Christ, the Divine and Eternal Word of God, in the man Jesus.

Christians believe that Christ is the ultimate special revelation of God to humanity, and the reason they believe this is because the Bible says so. The Bible is special revelation too. It gives us information about God that is not available through any other means. It enables people who would only know God through nature or logic as the abstract, transcendent God of Aquinas' Unmoved Mover, to understand that there is a personal, imminent God and Savior. It is through special revelation found in the Bible that one can know that Jesus is the Son of God, that the Holy Spirit exists, that God cares for every person, and of God's plan of salvation for humankind.

In the discussion of apologetics, Christians turn again and again to the Bible. In the same way that the one who comes to God must believe that He exists, so the one who comes to the Bible must believe that it is the Word of God, and that as such it is true and reliable. Jesus knew that the Bible was true, and He relied on what it said. When He was tempted by the devil, Jesus answered the great deceiver by saying "it is written"—and would quote the Bible. What is good enough for Jesus is good enough for Christians, and what Jesus felt was good enough for the devil must be good enough for atheists too.

Is the Bible reliable?

The Bible is the starting point for Christian apologetics. While natural revelation clearly has a place in apologetics, even this natural revelation must be interpreted through the "spectacles of Scripture." Natural revelation tells us there must be a God, the Bible tells us what kind of God He is. The written Scripture is how God has chosen to reveal Himself to humankind.

The Bible contains sixty-six books written in three languages (Hebrew, Aramaic, and Greek) by thirty-nine authors over a period of one thousand eight hundred years (1700 BC to 100 AD). The authors of these books include shepherds, prophets, kings, priests, poets, students, musicians, philosophers, fishermen, a tent maker who was trained as a theologian, and a doctor. It is full of poetry, proverbs, letters, laws, histories, prophecies, philosophy, and stories.

Despite being written by many different men and over a long time period, the entire Bible has remarkable unity. Imagine gathering five people in a room and asking their opinion on almost any subject. What are the chances that all five would agree? Probably extremely low. The chances of dozens of authors agreeing over a period of one thousand eight hundred years is astronomical. The one thing Bible authors agree on and that unites their different writings is the theme of salvation for humanity through Jesus Christ.

The reason for the unity within the Bible comes from the fact that the Bible really has only one author: God. While specific people throughout history wrote the books of the Bible, each person was inspired by God to write the words they did. *"All Scripture is God-breathed"* (2 Timothy 3:16 NIV) writes the Apostle Paul. The Word of God *"never had its origin in the human will, but prophets, though human, spoke from God as they were carried along by the Holy Spirit"* (2 Peter 1:21 NIV). So, while different men held the pens used to write the Scriptures, each man was guided by the Holy Spirit as he wrote.

If one does not believe the Bible is authoritative, then there is not much reason to refer to it in Christian apologetics. Christians do not read the Bible in the same way that other books are read. When people read the works of Homer or Shakespeare, they read them as literature. But the Bible is God's word to humanity. Before you can grasp the Bible, you must choose to believe it. If you are not willing to kneel when you read the Bible, you will never fully understand it.

There are many reasons why you can feel confident that the Bible is true. In this chapter and the one to follow, I will share seven reasons that I find compelling.

1. The Bible claims that what it says is true

The Bible claims to be a source of ultimate truth. The author of the Bible is none other than the all-knowing God Himself. If a book is written by God, one would expect to find that claim to be found within the book. On this point the Bible leaves its readers with no doubts, and it assures readers that, the Author being who He is, they can trust what is written. Here are a few things that the Bible has to say about itself as the Word of God:

God's Word will last forever. *"The grass withers, the flower fades, but the word of our God stands forever"* (Isaiah 40:8). *"But the word of the Lord endures forever"* (1 Peter 1:25). News stories change, histories are rewritten as the facts are reinterpreted, scientific opinions evolve, but century after century, God's Word endures the test of time.

God's Word is pure. *"The words of the Lord are pure words"* (Psalm 12:6). The Bible is inspired by the Holy Spirit. There is no hidden agenda or malice to be found in God's Word. It is pure and good for purifying the soul.

God's Word is useful. *"All Scripture is given by inspiration of God, and is profitable for doctrine, for reproof, for correction, for instruction in righteousness"* (2 Timothy 3:16). The Bible is useful for many things. It teaches us about God and about ourselves.

God's Word is powerful. *"For the word of God is living and powerful, and sharper than any two-edged sword, piercing even to the division of soul and spirit, and of joints and marrow, and is a discerner of the thoughts and intents of the heart"* (Hebrews 4:12). Nothing can change a human heart faster than the Bible. God's Word is like a mirror. When we hold it up to our faces and look, we see ourselves as we truly are. God's Word reveals our sinful nature and points us to a forgiving God.

2. The Bible was faithfully transmitted

While we do not have the original manuscripts of the Bible, there is far more evidence for the reliable transfer of the New Testament then there is for any other ancient manuscript. For example, Plato died in 347 BC, but the earliest manuscript of his writings is from 900 AD—a gap of one thousand two hundred years. Unfortunately, only seven copies of his manuscripts are known to be in existence. We have forty-nine copies of the writings of Aristotle, the student of Plato and tutor of Alexander the Great. His earliest surviving manuscript is from 1100 AD, one thousand four hundred years after he died. Homer wrote the *Iliad* around 900 BC. The earliest Homeric manuscript is from 400 BC, five hundred years after he wrote it. We have 643 known copies of his writings. The earliest biography that is available about the life of Buddha was written over six hundred years after his death.

In contrast, the earliest manuscripts of the New Testament are dated to around 130 AD, less than one hundred years after the Apostles penned the originals. It is likely that the entire New Testament was written during the first century. When Paul talks about the reality of the resurrection of Jesus (1 Corinthians 15:4), he is writing only twenty years after the crucifixion took place (around 30 AD). There is one fragment of the Gospel of John that might date to the late first or early second centuries—within years of the Apostle's death (around 96 AD).[1]

When the New Testament was being written, there were people still alive who had been eyewitnesses to the events of Jesus' life, death, and resurrection. The New Testament is not a group of legends passed down over centuries; it is living history recorded by participants in the events.

Plus, there are, not hundreds, but thousands of copies of the New Testament dating from the early centuries of our era. There are almost six thousand copies of the New Testament in the Greek language, and another twenty-one thousand copies in other languages—including

Syriac, Latin, Coptic, and Aramaic texts. While the copies are many, significantly, the differences between them are few. There is less than 0.5 percent variation between all early texts of the New Testament books. Most of these variations can be accounted for by differences in spelling, word repetition, or word omission.[2] These variations can be corrected easily by comparing the vast number of manuscripts that we have available.

There is far more evidence for the accuracy and validity of the New Testament and its record of the life and words of Jesus than there is for any other historical figure or manuscript from His time period. The comparatively short time periods between the lives of Christ and the Apostles and the earliest manuscripts of New Testament writings means there is very little time in which their words could be distorted or their message compromised. While only seven copies of Plato's writings are the basis of modern texts of his works—and those copies are far-distanced from his own period—few scholars question Plato's existence or doubt the validity of his writings. If one rejects the evidence for the New Testament manuscripts and the words of Jesus, then one must equally reject as accurate the writings of Plato, Aristotle, and Homer. Conversely, to be willing to accept the works of these authors as representative of what they said or wrote, the reader of the Bible can be so much more confident that the words of the New Testament, the words of Jesus, have been faithfully transmitted down the centuries.

3. The Bible has been found to be accurate

The writers of the Bible strove to be accurate in what they wrote. For example, Luke, the writer of the *Gospel of Luke* and the *Acts of the Apostles*, carefully investigated the life of Jesus and the history of the early church that he records. This is how Luke explains his careful historical research:

> *Many have undertaken to draw up an account of the things that have been fulfilled among us, just as they were handed down to us by those who from the first were eyewitnesses and servants of the word. With this in mind, since I myself have carefully investigated*

everything from the beginning, I too decided to write an orderly account for you, most excellent Theophilus, so that you may know the certainty of the things you have been taught. (Luke 1:1-4 NIV)

Luke traveled with the Apostle Paul, and it is likely that as he traveled, he interviewed eyewitnesses to the life of Jesus. His detailed writing indicates that he had access to primary sources, including Mary, the mother of Jesus. Of the Gospel writers, he is the one who gives the most detailed account of the nativity. He mentions Mary twelve times—more than any of the other Gospel writers—and he includes the story of Elizabeth, the cousin of Mary, who gave birth to John the Baptist. For his account of the history of the early Church in *Acts*, besides his own first-hand knowledge of many of the events he records, he would have been able to get first-hand accounts from the other Apostles and personalities of the early Church that his travels and associations brought him in contact with.

Where the Bible records historical detail, it has been found to be accurate in its record. Luke accurately records details of the people, places, dates, and events he writes about. The famous archaeologist, Sir William Ramsay, traveled to Asia Minor to prove that Luke was an inferior historian. However, after retracing the steps of Paul's missionary journeys, he concluded: "Luke is a historian of the first rank; not merely are his statements of fact trustworthy, he is possessed of the true historic sense; in short, this author should be placed along with the greatest of historians."[3] A.N. Sherwin-White looked at Luke's references to thirty-two countries, fifty-four cities, and nine islands, and found no mistakes.[4] Since Luke was careful to accurately record names, places, and dates, we can be confident that he was also accurate in recording the facts of Jesus' life.

Likewise, the many historical details, including of kings and pharaohs and places and customs, that are found in the Old Testament prove the Bible's accuracy.[5] Consider the following twenty-five archeological and historical discoveries that support the Biblical record:

1. The oldest known inscription of the name "Yahweh" was written by the Egyptian Pharaoh Amenhotep III c. 1400 BC. The inscription refers to a nomadic group of people who worshiped "Yahweh" (undoubtedly, the Israelites). It was found in Soleb, a town in modern day Sudan.

2. The Merneptah Stela was carved c. 1210 BC and contains the earliest reference to "Israel" in hieroglyphs. It was found in Thebes in 1896.

3. The Tel Dan Stela was written in Aramaic in the ninth century BC. It refers to the "House of David." It was found on the site of the ancient city of Dan in northern Israel in 1993. This artifact is now in the Israel Museum.

4. The invasion of Pharaoh Shishak into the land of Israel (c. 925 BC) mentioned in 1 Kings 14:25 has been confirmed by wall carvings in the Karnak Temple complex in Egypt.

5. The Kurkh Monolith is a seven-foot-tall limestone monument that was discovered in 1861 in Kurkh, Turkey. It was carved c. 852 BC by the ancient Assyrians and refers to a battle with Ahab, king of Israel, who is frequently mentioned in the Bible (1 Kings 16-22).

6. The Moabite Stone is a four-foot-tall monument made of black basalt that mentions the Israelite King Omri and Moabite King Mesha (both mentioned in 1 and 2 Kings). It also refers to "Yahweh." Carved in the Moabite language c. 835 BC, this primary historical source is now in the Louvre.

7. The Obelisk of Shalmaneser III, a six-and-a-half foot-tall monument in black limestone from c. 827 BC, pictures an Israelite king bowing to the king of Assyria. The cuneiform text on the obelisk reads, "Tribute of Jehu, son of Omri." Both kings are mentioned in the books of 1 and 2 Kings.

8. In 1904, a jasper seal (eighth century BC) was discovered at Megiddo that reads, "belonging to Shema, servant of Jeroboam." Two Israelite

kings by this name are mentioned in the Bible (1 Kings 12-14; 2 Kings 14).

9. What is referred to as "Hezekiah's tunnel" was built by that King of Judah in 700 BC to bring water into Jerusalem (2 Kings 20:20). The tunnel has been found with an ancient Hebrew inscription.

10. The Sennacherib Prism mentions Sennacherib's attack on King Hezekiah that is recorded in 2 Kings 19:9. The prism was found in 1919 and is now in the Oriental Institute Museum at the University of Chicago.

11. The siege of Lachish, mentioned in 2 Kings 18-19 was documented on a wall relief found in Nineveh. This relief is now in the British Museum.

12. 2 Kings 19:37 mentions an Assyrian king named Esarhaddon. A ten-foot monument commemorating his victory in Egypt was made in the seventh century BC, and was found in 1881 in Zinjirli, Turkey. It can be seen in the Museum of the Ancient Near East, Pergamum Museum, Berlin.

13. The Esarhaddon Prism, from c. 673 BC, is named after this same Assyrian king. The prism mentions "Manasseh king of Judea" who can be read about in 2 Kings 20 and 2 Chronicles 33.

14. Pharaoh Tirhakah is mentioned in the Bible in 2 Kings 19:9 and Isaiah 37:9. A wall carving that has a picture of the Pharaoh from the seventh century BC was found in the Edifice of Tirhakah in the Egyptian city of Luxor.

15. According to 2 Kings 25:29-30, King Jehoiachin of Judah was given a regular alliance from the king of Babylon. This historical detail is confirmed by a clay tablet written in the Akkadian language (c. 595-570 BC) that was found in Babylon in 1900.

16. Belshazzar, a Babylonian king, is mentioned in the Book of Daniel—see chapters 5 and 8. Clay cylinders in the Akkadian language that mention his name were found in the city of Ur in the nineteenth century and can now be seen in the British Museum.

17. A silver scroll written in 600 BC contains the oldest known quote from Hebrew scripture taken from Numbers 6:24-26. It was found in 1979 in Jerusalem and is now in the Israel Museum.

18. The Dead Sea Scrolls were found in 1947 and 1956 at Qumran near the Dead Sea. They were originally written c. 200 BC to AD 70. Portions of every book in the Old Testament (except Esther) were found. The nearly complete text of the book of Isaiah proves that it was accurately transmitted for more than a thousand years.

19. King Herod, who plays a significant role in the narratives around the nativity and childhood of Jesus, is a well-documented historical figure, infamous for his ruthlessness. The execution of John the Baptist, recorded in Matthew 14, is also mentioned by the Jewish historian Josephus.

20. The emperors of Roman history are accurately recorded in the New Testament including Augustus (27 BC- AD 14; Luke 2:1), Tiberius (14-37 AD; Luke 3:1), and Claudius (41-54 AD; Luke 11:28, 18:2).

21. A house, thought to be the home of the Apostle Peter, was found under the ruins of a church in the village of Capernaum during excavations in 1968 and 1998.

22. The pool of Siloam, mentioned in John 9:7, was found in 2004.

23. A slab of limestone from 30 AD and found in 1961 on the site of the Roman port of Caesarea Maritima (in Israel) mentions "Tiberium Pontius Pilate Prefect of Judea." This is undoubtedly the same Pontius Pilate who sent Jesus to his death (Matthew 27).

24. Mars Hill, where Paul preached in Acts 17, can still be found in the center of Athens, Greece.

25. The ancient theater of Ephesus where Paul preached in Acts 19:29 can still be seen today. It seats up to twenty-four thousand people. His preaching of the Gospel caused a riot as the people of Ephesus responded to him by chanting "Great is Artemis of the Ephesians!" (Acts 19:34). The importance of the ancient city as a site for the worship of this pagan goddess is well documented in history and the archeological record. A nine-foot-tall marble statue of the goddess can be seen at the museum in Ephesus.

Instances of archeological and historical evidence for the accuracy of the Bible abound. The above are only a few examples of why the Bible is reliable where it documents history. Since the books of the Bible are accurate in the areas we can check, then this indicates a strong possibility that they are also accurate in the areas we cannot check.

The Bible is accurate in the area of science. The Bible is not written as a science textbook but it does convey scientific truth in many areas. As Oswald Chambers, the author of the classic Christian Devotional, *My Utmost for His Highest*, wrote: "If the Bible agreed with modern science, it would soon be out of date, because…modern science is bound to change." Nonetheless, the Bible does contain many scientific concepts that agree with modern science. For example:[6]

The earth is a sphere. Many different cultures used to think the earth was flat, but the Bible describes the true shape of the earth in Isaiah 40:22.

The construction of the cosmos. At one time, people in different cultures—Hindu, Chinese, and native American—believed the earth was supported on the back of a great turtle. Greek mythology gave this role to the Titan, Atlas. The ancient Biblical book of Job states that the earth and the cosmos are suspended in nothing (Job 26:7).

The world under the oceans. Long before scientists were able to explore the oceans using submarines, the Bible describes underwater valleys (Psalm 18:15) and fountains and springs in the depths (Job 38:16).

The hydrologic cycle. Referring to how water changes from a vapor in the atmosphere to become precipitation on land and water and then evaporates once again, Ecclesiastes 1:6-7 is understood to be an ancient observation of this scientifically important cycle.

Significantly, science owes a great debt to the Bible and Christian theology. The Bible teaches that the universe is orderly because it was created by a God of order, who is not the author of confusion (1 Corinthians 14:33). This theological understanding of the world contributed to the beginning of modern science in the Renaissance. Other gods of the ancient world, like Zeus and Thor, were powerful, but they were capricious rather than consistent and orderly. The Biblical God provided a philosophical foundation for science to flourish. It is not an accident that Galileo was both a theologian and a scientist.

When I consider the Bible—what it says about God, how accurately it has been transmitted, that its historical details are valid, and that it is scientifically consistent—my confidence in the truth of the evidence it presents is only strengthened. And on this point the Bible is certain:

God is THERE!

PROOF

CHAPTER 6

Scripture Proof 2—More Evidence from the Bible

Premise A: *The Bible says God exists.*

Premise B: *Human history has proved that the Bible is reliable.*

Conclusion: *Therefore, God exists.*

Let's continue the discussion of why Christians trust the Bible as a source of evidence for God by considering the last four of the seven reasons why I find the Bible to be a compelling source of truth.

4. The Bible is internally consistent—consider the prophecies about Jesus

Prophecy is an example of special revelation, which, as discussed in the previous chapter, refers to things about God that could only be known if God Himself revealed them to us. The Bible contains numerous prophecies about how Jesus, the Son of God, would come, what He would do when He came, and how He would be a Savior for sinful mankind. These prophecies were not written by one person at one time, but by different people over the course of the 1500 years before Christ came. The authors of the Old Testament were Jewish, and it was through them that God communicated the promise of a Savior. The

Jews carefully passed down the prophecies about this Messiah who was to come. Like the early Christians with the New Testament, the Jewish scribes were meticulous in transmitting the Old Testament scriptures that contained these precious promises. As they transcribed them, they counted every word and every letter in every word to ensure that any changes or errors were caught. In these Old Testament scriptures there are over three hundred prophecies about the Messiah that were fulfilled in the details of the life of Jesus. Consider the following fifteen instances of Old Testament prophecies and their fulfillment:

The Messiah would be the seed of a woman. Prophecy: *"I will put enmity between you and the woman, And between your seed and her Seed; He shall bruise your head, And you shall bruise His heel."* (Genesis 3:15).

Fulfillment by Jesus: *"But when the fullness of the time had come, God sent forth His Son, born of a woman"* (Galatians 4:4).

The Messiah would be a descendant of the Old Testament patriarch Abraham. Prophecy: *"In you [Abraham] all the families of the earth shall be blessed"* (Genesis 12:3).

Fulfillment by Jesus: *"The book of the genealogy of Jesus Christ…the Son of Abraham"* (Matthew 1:1).

The Messiah would be from the tribe of Judah (one of the twelve tribes of Israel). Prophecy: *"The scepter shall not depart from Judah, nor a lawgiver from between his feet, until Shiloh comes; and to Him shall be the obedience of the people"* (Genesis 49:10).

Fulfillment by Jesus: *"Now Jesus Himself began His ministry at about thirty years of age, being (as was supposed) the son of Joseph, the son of Heli"* (Luke 3:23). *"For it is evident that our Lord arose from Judah, of which tribe Moses spoke nothing concerning priesthood"* (Hebrews 7:14).

The Messiah would be a descendant of King David. Prophecy: *"When your days [David's] are fulfilled and you rest with your fathers, I will set up your seed after you, who will come from your body, and I will* *establish his kingdom"* (2 Samuel 7:12). *"'Behold, the days are coming,"* says the Lord, *'That I will raise to David a Branch of righteousness; A King shall reign and prosper, And execute judgment and righteousness in the earth'"* (Jeremiah 23:5).

Fulfillment by Jesus: *"The book of the genealogy of Jesus Christ, the Son of David…"* (Matthew 1:1).

The Messiah would be born to a virgin. Prophecy: *"Therefore the Lord Himself will give you a sign: Behold, the virgin shall conceive and bear a Son"* (Isaiah 7:14).

Fulfillment by Jesus: *"Then the angel said to her, 'Do not be afraid, Mary, for you have found favor with God. And behold you will conceive in your womb and bring forth a Son, and shall call His name Jesus' […] Then Mary said to the angel, 'How can this be, since I do not know a man?'"* (Luke 1:30-31, 34). *"Now the birth of Jesus Christ was as follows: After His mother Mary was betrothed to Joseph, before they came together, she was found with child of the Holy Spirit"* (Matthew 1:18).

The Messiah would be born in Bethlehem. Prophecy: *"But you, Bethlehem Ephrathah, Though you are little among the thousands of Judah, Yet out of you shall come forth to Me The One to be Ruler in Israel"* (Micah 5:2).

Fulfillment by Jesus: *"Now after Jesus was born in Bethlehem of Judea in the days of Herod the king, behold, wise men from the East came to Jerusalem"* (Matthew 2:1). *"Joseph also went up from Galilee, out of the city of Nazareth, into Judea, to the city of David, which is called Bethlehem, because he was of the house and lineage of David, to be registered with Mary, his betrothed wife, who was with child. So it was, that while they were there, the days were completed for her to be delivered. And she brought forth her firstborn Son"* (Luke 2:4-7).

The Messiah would perform great miracles. Prophecy: *"Then the eyes of the blind shall be opened, and the ears of the deaf shall be unstopped.*

Then the lame shall leap like a deer, and the tongue of the dumb sing" (Isaiah 35:5-6).

Fulfillment by Jesus: *"Jesus went about all Galilee, teaching in their synagogues, preaching the gospel of the kingdom, and healing all kinds of sickness and all kinds of disease among the people"* (Matthew 4:23).

The Messiah would be rejected by His own people. Prophecy: *"He is despised and rejected by men, A Man of sorrows and acquainted with grief. And we hid, as it were, our faces from Him; He was despised, and we did not esteem Him"* (Isaiah 53:3).

Fulfillment by Jesus: *"He was in the world, and the world was made through Him, and the world did not know Him. He came to His own, and His own did not receive Him"* (John 1:10-11). *"For even His brothers did not believe in Him"* (John 7:5). *"Have any of the rulers or the Pharisees believed in Him?"* (John 7:48).

The Messiah would be betrayed by a close friend. Prophecy: *"Even my own familiar friend in whom I trusted, who ate my bread, has lifted up his heel against me"* (Psalm 41:9).

Fulfillment by Jesus: Jesus said, *"Most assuredly, I say to you, one of you will betray Me"* (John 13:21).

The Messiah would be betrayed for thirty pieces of silver. Prophecy: *"So they weighed out for my wages thirty pieces of silver"* (Zechariah 11:12).

Fulfillment by Jesus: *"Then one of the twelve, called Judas Iscariot, went to the chief priests and said, 'What are you willing to give me if I deliver Him to you?' And they counted out to him thirty pieces of silver"* (Matthew 26:15).

The Messiah's hands and feet would be pierced. Prophecy: *"... They pierced My hands and My feet"* (Psalm 22:16). *"Then they will look on Me whom they pierced"* (Zechariah 12:10).

Fulfillment by Jesus: *"And when they had come to the place called Calvary, there they crucified Him"* (Luke 23:33).

The Messiah would be crucified with thieves. Prophecy: *"And He was numbered with the transgressors"* (Isaiah 53:12).

Fulfillment by Jesus: *"With Him they also crucified two robbers, one on His right and the other on His left. So the Scripture was fulfilled which says, 'And He was numbered with the transgressors'"* (Mark 15:27-28).

The Messiah's clothes would be gambled for. Prophecy: *"They divide My garments among them, And for My clothing they cast lots"* (Psalm 22:18).

Fulfillment by Jesus: *"Then the soldiers, when they had crucified Jesus, took His garments and made four parts, to each soldier a part, and also the tunic. Now the tunic was without seam, woven from the top in one piece. They said therefore among themselves, 'Let us not tear it, but cast lots for it, whose it shall be,' that the Scripture might be fulfilled which says: 'They divided My garments among them, And for My clothing they cast lots.' Therefore the soldiers did these things"* (John 19:23-24).

The Messiah would be buried in a rich man's tomb. Prophecy: *"And they made His grave with the wicked, But with the rich at His death"* (Isaiah 53:9).

Fulfillment by Jesus: *"Now when evening had come, there came a rich man from Arimathea, named Joseph, who himself had also become a disciple of Jesus. This man went to Pilate and asked for the body of Jesus. Then Pilate commanded the body to be given to him. When Joseph had taken the body, he wrapped it in a clean linen cloth, and laid it in his new tomb which he had hewn out of the rock; and he rolled a large stone against the door of the tomb, and departed"* (Matthew 27:57-60).

The Messiah would rise from the dead. Prophecy: *"For You will not leave my soul in Sheol, nor will You allow Your Holy One to see corruption"* (Psalm 16:10).

Fulfillment by Jesus: *"He, foreseeing this, spoke concerning the resurrection of the Christ, that His soul was not left in Hades, nor did His flesh see corruption"* (Acts 2:31). *"But he said to them, 'Do not be alarmed. You seek Jesus of Nazareth, who was crucified. He is risen! He is not here. See the place where they laid Him'"* (Mark 16:6).

While it might seem that a person could fulfill prophecy by accident, the probability that a person could coincidentally fulfill this number of prophecies is nearly impossible. It has been calculated that the mathematical chances of a man fulfilling just eight of these prophecies would be 1 in 100,000,000,000,000,000.[1] This number exponentially increases with every additional prophecy fulfilled. Peter Stoner, a scientist and mathematician, calculated that the probability of a person fulfilling forty-eight of the Old Testament prophecies about the Messiah would be one chance in a trillion, trillion, trillion, trillion, trillion, trillion, trillion, trillion, trillion, trillion, trillion, trillion, trillion. Such a number is basically incomprehensible. As big as this number is, consider that Jesus didn't complete just forty-eight prophecies—His life fulfilled three hundred prophetic details from the Old Testament.

The New Testament shows that Jesus Christ is the fulfillment of the Old Testament prophecies. The internal consistency is so improbable that it serves as proof of the divine origins of the book. The miraculous fulfillment of Old Testament prophecies by Jesus convinced many Jews to join the early church. The clear evidence that He did so continues to convince people that Jesus is the Messiah and the Son of God and leads them to put their hope and trust in Him.

5. The Bible is full of wisdom

The Bible contains much more than prophecy. It is a group of books that includes history, poetry, prophecy, law, letters, and wisdom literature. The wisdom literature of the Bible contains a great deal of ethical wisdom—principles and advice for daily living and how to live the best life. One book of the Bible that contains plentiful examples of this kind of wisdom is the book of Proverbs. This book tells us: *"Blessed are those who find wisdom, those who gain understanding..."* (Proverbs

3:13 NIV). Besides Proverbs, wisdom can be found in other books of the Bible—the "Sermon on the Mount" (Matthew 5-7) and the Epistle of James are examples of wisdom literature in the New Testament. Wisdom from the Bible covers topics that include:

* The value of integrity (Proverbs 28:6).
* The importance of obeying one's parents.
* Advice for remaining teachable (Proverbs 10:23).
* The danger of arrogance (Proverbs 14:16; 30:32).
* The importance of listening to advice (Proverbs 12:15).
* A foundation for morality—found in the Ten Commandments (Exodus 20:1-17).
* Best practices for how to treat other people.
* The importance of choosing good friends
* Practical tips for maintaining healthy sexual relationships.
* Warnings about being lazy and the poverty it leads to (Proverbs 10:4).
* Instructions for how to get to heaven (Romans 10:9-10).

The above is a small sampling of the wisdom of the Bible that has been proved to be true across generations and cultures. Ultimately, the wisdom found in the Bible comes from God who is the source of all wisdom. It also tells us where wisdom begins: *"The fear of the Lord is the beginning of wisdom and the knowledge of the Holy One is understanding"* (Proverbs 9:10). This simply means that knowing that God is there is the starting point to living wisely. But *"The fool says in his heart, 'There is no God'"* (Psalm 53:1). If you feel that you could use more wisdom in your life, open the Bible. God wants you to know how to live your life to the fullest. The Bible promises, *"If any of you lacks wisdom, you should ask God, who gives generously to all without finding fault, and it will be given to you"* (James 1:5 NIV).

Many people have discovered the wisdom found in this tremendous book—people who have given shape to history and our world.

6. No book has as many character witnesses and recommendations as the Bible

A person who is on trial, as part of making the case for his innocence, can call on "character witnesses" to defend him. These witnesses are friends or notable community members, who, on taking the stand, give testimony to the good character of the one on trial. Under oath to tell "the truth, the whole truth, and nothing but the truth," they wax eloquent about the nobleness of the accused's character and talk about all the good things their friend has done. In a way, the Bible has its character witnesses too, and they are not a few. Significantly, those who have come forward in its defense are among the noblest and most respected figures in human history—many people who have shaped our world have stood up to give evidence of the wisdom, truth, value, and power of the Word of God.

The testimony of founding fathers and presidents of the United States

The United States of America was founded on the principles of Christianity. Many of the original settlers came to the shores of this land looking for religious freedom. America's Founding Fathers (and mothers) had deep knowledge of the Old and New Testaments. Their writings and speeches abound with references to the Bible. The Declaration of Independence proclaims that humankind is *"endowed by their Creator with certain unalienable Rights, that among these are Life, Liberty and the pursuit of Happiness."* The first amendment to the Bill of Rights in the Constitution guarantees freedom of religion. The three branches of the U.S. government (Executive, Legislative, and Judicial) are derived from Isaiah 33:22 which says that the Lord is our Judge, our Lawgiver, and our King. American history is full of our greatest minds explaining the importance of the Bible.

"It is impossible to rightly govern the world without God and the Bible."—George Washington, 1st President

"The Bible is worth all other books which have ever been printed."—Patrick Henry, Founding Father

"The Bible is the best of all books, for it is the Word of God and teaches us the way to be happy in this world and in the next. Continue therefore to read it and to regulate your life by its precepts."—John Jay, first Chief Justice of the Supreme Court

"I have always said that a studious perusal of the sacred volume will make better citizens, better fathers, and better husbands."—Thomas Jefferson, 3rd President

"We have staked the whole future of American civilization, not upon the power of government, far from it. We have staked the future of all of our political institutions upon the capacity of mankind for self-government; upon the capacity of each and all of us to govern ourselves, to control ourselves, to sustain ourselves according to The Ten Commandments of God."—James Madison, 4th President

"So great is my veneration for the Bible that the earlier my children begin to read it the more confident will be my hope that they will prove useful citizens of their country and respectable members of society. I have for many years made it a practice to read through the Bible once every year."—John Quincy Adams, 6th President

"[The Bible] is the rock on which our Republic rests."—Andrew Jackson, 7th President

"If there is anything in my thoughts or style to commend, the credit is due my parents for instilling in me an early love of the Scriptures. If we abide by the principles taught in the Bible, our country will go on prospering and to prosper; but if we and our posterity neglect its instructions and authority, no man can tell how sudden a catastrophe may overwhelm us and bury all our glory in profound obscurity"—Daniel Webster, American Secretary of State under three presidents

"In regards to this great Book [the Bible], I have but to say it is the best gift God has given to man. All the good the Savior gave to the world was communicated through this Book. But for it we could not know right from

wrong. All things most desirable for man's welfare, here and hereafter, are found portrayed in it."—Abraham Lincoln, 16th President

"I am profitably engaged in reading the Bible. Take all of this Book that you can by reason and the balance by faith, and you will live and die a better man. It is the best Book which God has given to man."—Abraham Lincoln, 16th President

"It is necessary for the welfare of the nation that men's lives be based on the principles of the Bible. No man, educated or uneducated, can afford to be ignorant of the Bible."—Theodore Roosevelt, 26th President

"I am sorry for men who do not read the Bible every day. I wonder why they deprive themselves of the strength and pleasure"—Woodrow Wilson, 28th President

"[The United States is] founded on the principles of Christianity."—Franklin D. Roosevelt, 32nd President

"The fundamental basis of this Nation's law was given to Moses on the Mount. The fundamental basis of our Bill of Rights comes from the teachings which we get from Exodus and St. Matthew, from Isaiah and St. Paul."—Harry S. Truman, 33rd President

"Without God there could be no American form of government, nor an American way of life. Recognition of the Supreme Being is the first, the most basic, expression of Americanism. Thus, the founding fathers of America saw it, and thus with God's help, it will continue to be."—Dwight D. Eisenhower, 34th President

"Within the covers of the Bible are the answers for all the problems men face. Of the many influences that have shaped the United States into a distinctive nation and people, none may be said to be more fundamental and enduring than the Bible."—Ronald Reagan, 40th President

The recommendations of other world leaders

To the testimony of such significant leaders in the history of our own country, we can add the evidence of great rulers and statesmen of Europe who have also felt the Bible's tremendous influence.

"The Bible is no mere book, but a Living Creature, with a power that conquers all that oppose it."—Napoleon I, Emperor of France

"Tell your prince that this Book (the Bible) is the secret of England's greatness."—Queen Victoria, to an African ambassador who had asked why England was such a great nation

"We rest with assurance upon 'The Impregnable Rock of Holy Scripture'."—Sir Winston Churchill, Prime Minister of Great Britain, and first person to be made an honorary citizen of the United States

"To what greater inspiration and counsel can we turn than to the imperishable truth to be found in this Treasure House, the Bible?"—Queen Elizabeth II

What scientists say about the Bible and Christianity

In modern times, it is often said that science and religion do not mix. But the history of science is full of scientists who were inspired in their scientific quest by their knowledge of the Bible and who found no problem with reconciling their scientific discoveries with their Christian faith. Indeed, it was the belief in a Creator that pushed early scientists to discover the immutable laws of His creation. Without Christianity, it is doubtful there ever would have been a scientific revolution.

"There are two books laid before us to study, to prevent our falling into error: first, the volume of the Scriptures, which reveal the will of God; then the volume of the Creatures, which express His power."—Francis Bacon, who helped to establish the "Scientific Method"

"We account the Scriptures of God to be the most sublime philosophy. I find more sure marks of authenticity in the Bible than in any profane

history whatsoever. No sciences are better attested than the religion of the Bible."—Sir Isaac Newton, responsible for the discovery of gravity and the creation of Calculus

"*O God, I am thinking Thy thoughts after Thee.*"—Johannes Kepler, astronomer and cosmologist

"*The more I study nature, the more I stand amazed at the work of the Creator.*"—Louis Pasteur, biologist and chemist who discovered the principles of vaccination

"*The conduct of God, who disposes all things kindly, is to put religion into the mind by reason, and into the heart by grace. But to will to put it into the mind and heart by force and threats is not to put religion there, but terror.*"—Blaise Pascal, mathematician and physicist, who developed theory of probability

"*It is His work,*" he reminded them; "*and He alone carried me thus far through all my trials and enabled me to triumph over the obstacles, physical and moral, which opposed me. 'Not unto us, but to Thy name, O Lord, be all the praise'.*"—Samuel Morse, inventor

"*When with bold telescopes I survey the old and newly discovered stars and planets; when with excellent microscopes I discern the inimitable subtlety of nature's curious workmanship; and when, in a word, by the help of anatomical knives, and the light of chemical furnaces, I study the book of nature I find myself oftentimes reduced to exclaim with the Psalmist, How manifold are Thy works, O Lord! In wisdom hast Thou made them all!*"—Robert Boyle, chemist, physicist and inventor

"*Finite man cannot begin to comprehend an omnipresent, omniscient, omnipotent, and infinite God...I find it best to accept God through faith, as an intelligent will, perfect in goodness and wisdom, revealing Himself through His creation.*"—Werner Von Braun, aerospace engineer and rocket scientist

"The flowers' leaves…serve as bridal beds which the Creator has so gloriously arranged, adorned with such noble bed curtains, and perfumed with so many soft scents that the bridegroom with his bride might there celebrate their nuptials with so much the greater solemnity."—Carl Linnaeus, biologist and zoologist who is called the "Father of Taxonomy"

Philosophers support the Bible

History's greatest philosophical minds have wrestled with the existence of God, and many philosophers have decided to trust in the God of the Bible.

"The Bible is one of the greatest blessings bestowed by God on the children of men. It has God for its Author, Salvation for its end, and Truth without any mixture for its matter. It is all pure, all sincere; nothing too much; nothing wanting."—John Locke, English philosopher

"The existence of the Bible, as a book for the people, is the greatest benefit which the human race has ever experienced. Every attempt to belittle it is a crime against humanity."—Immanuel Kant, German philosopher

"The Bible is very easy to understand. But we Christians are a bunch of scheming swindlers. We pretend to be unable to understand it because we know very well that the minute we understand, we are obliged to act accordingly."—Soren Kierkegaard, Danish philosopher

What famous authors and poets say about the Bible

Scattered throughout Western literature are allusions and references to the Bible. In times past, children learned to read from the pages of the Holy Book.

"Education is useless without the Bible. The Bible was America's basic textbook in all fields. God's Word, contained in the Bible, has furnished all necessary rules to direct our conduct."—Noah Webster, author of *Webster's Dictionary*

"Western literature has been more influenced by the Bible than any other book."—Thomas B. Macaulay, English historian

"The most learned, acute, and diligent student cannot, in the longest life, obtain an entire knowledge of the BIBLE. The more deeply he works the mine, the richer and more abundant he finds the ore."—Sir Walter Scott, Scottish poet and novelist

"Bible reading is an education in itself."—Lord Tennyson, poet laureate of Great Britain

"The New Testament is the very best book that ever was or ever will be known in the world."—Charles Dickens, English novelist

"England has two books, the Bible and Shakespeare. England made Shakespeare, but the Bible made England."—Victor Hugo, French poet, novelist, and dramatist

Testimony from preachers and theologians

Of course, the Bible has inspired preachers and theologians. What do they have to say about the Word of God?

"The Holy Scriptures are our letters from home."—Saint Augustine (of Hippo), Early Christian theologian and author

"For some years now I have read through the Bible twice every year. If you picture the Bible to be a mighty tree and every word a little branch, I have shaken every one of these branches because I wanted to know what it was and what it meant."—Martin Luther, leader of the Protestant Reformation

"I am a creature of a day. I am a spirit come from God, and returning to God. I want to know one thing: the way to heaven. God Himself has condescended to teach me the way. He has written it down in a book. Oh, give me that book! At any price give me the book of God. Let me be a man of one book."—John Wesley, founder of the Methodist movement

"The vigor of our spiritual life will be in exact proportion to the place held by the Bible in our life and thoughts."—George Mueller, Christian evangelist and missionary

"God's Word is as good as He is. There is an old saying that a man is as good as his word. Well, God is as good as His Word. His character is behind what He has said."—J. Vernon McGee, Presbyterian minister

While so many notable character witnesses attest to the trustworthiness of the Bible, millions and millions of people who have no claim to fame could do so as well. The Bible is the best-selling book in history. There is no other book that has influenced more people or been responsible for changing more lives. The Bible is the foundational text of Judeo-Christian society. Without the Bible, the morals and values of Western society and democracy would not exist. The sheer number of lives the Bible has impacted prove it is a divine book.

7. The Bible has changed my life

The final reason I believe the Bible is true is because the Bible has shaped my life. I believe the Bible is inspired because it inspires me. I live my life according to the Word of God. Because of the foundational moral teachings of the Bible, I have an authoritative guide to what is right and what is wrong. Because of God's Word, I am committed to stay married to my wife. Because of God's Word, I preach the Gospel. Because of God's Word, I love others. Because of God's Word, I live a life of faith. Because of God's Word, I trust in the goodness of God. Because of God's Word, I believe in divine healing. Because of the Word of God, I am who I am by the grace of God. While I make no claim to be a perfect person or a model of how to live, I know that the Word of God challenges me to be a better person every day. Where I make mistakes, the Bible shows me how to change—and not just by trying harder to be a better person, but by letting Jesus Christ be the Lord of my life. The Apostle Paul put it this way: *"I have been crucified with Christ; it is no longer I who live, but Christ lives in me: and the life which I now live in the flesh I live by faith in the Son of God, who loved me and gave Himself for me"* (Galatians 2:20).

If the Bible were on trial, the mountain of evidence for its reliability should be sufficient to convince an impartial jury of its truth and dependability. When I read the Bible, written over a period of eighteen hundred years by its thirty-nine authors, and see it proclaim with perfect unity God's goodness and love toward mankind, I say:

"Yes, God is THERE!"

CHAPTER 7

Supernatural Proof—Evidence
from Miracles

Premise A: *If miracles occur, they would require supernatural agency.*

Premise B: *Miracles occur.*

Conclusion: *Therefore, supernatural agency exists. This agency we call God.*

A miracle is an extraordinary event that transcends natural law and is beyond human capacity to explain or duplicate. One scholar defined a miracle as "a work wrought by God's power for God's purpose by means beyond the reach of man." The word "miracle" is derived from the Latin word *mirari*, which means, "to wonder." In other words, a miracle is an event which causes wonder. If there is a God who is maximally great—all-good and all-powerful—the occurrence of miracles, however wonderful, would be reasonable and plausible. The question then remains: Do miracles really occur? Does God still do miracles today?

The answer to these questions is "Yes!" and these miracles prove that God is real. In a Newsweek Poll, 84% of Americans say they believe in miracles. 79% believe that the miracles described in the Bible occurred.

63% claim to know someone who experienced a miracle and 48% claim to have personally experienced a miracle![1]

Miracles are an integral part of Christianity and of God's interaction with people

The Bible is a history of miracles because every interaction of God with humankind is a supernatural occurrence. The Bible records how God split the Red Sea so that Moses could lead the people of Israel through it on dry land. The prophet Elijah was fed by ravens who brought him food twice a day because God made them do so. Jonah records how he was swallowed by a big fish divinely appointed for the task. Shadrach, Meshach, and Abednego were preserved unharmed in a raging fiery furnace, while those who looked on saw one, like the Son of God, walking in the flames with them. These and other miraculous events recorded in the Old Testament were preambles to the central miracle of Scripture: Jesus.

Jesus performed many miracles during His ministry, and in performing them, He proved He was none other than the Messiah, the Son of God and the Savior of sinful humanity. When the religious leaders of His day said that He could not forgive sins—because doing so was an act reserved only for God—Jesus healed the paralyzed man as proof of His ability to do what only God could do (Matthew 9:6). When John the Baptist asked for proof that Jesus was the Messiah, Jesus referred him to the miracles He had done: *"Go back and report to John what you hear and see: The blind receive sight, the lame walk, those who have leprosy are cleansed, the deaf hear, the dead are raised, and the good news is proclaimed to the poor"* (Matthew 11:4-5).

Not only were miracles an essential part of Christ's ministry, but He was Himself a miracle. Jesus' birth was miraculous: Mary, His mother, become pregnant with Him by the power of the Holy Spirit. Not only was His birth miraculous, His resurrection after He died on the cross was even more miraculous. The resurrection of Jesus was well attested. He was seen by individuals, by small groups of people, and by as many as 500 people at once in the 40 days between His resurrection and His ascension to heaven.

When the Apostles of Jesus performed miracles, they claimed the miracles were evidence of the resurrection and saving power of the divine Lord they preached about:

> *Peter…responded to the people: "Men of Israel, why do you marvel at this* [referring to the miracle of the healing of the lame man at the Gate Beautiful]*? Or why look so intently at us, as though by our own power or godliness we had made this man walk? The God of Abraham, Isaac, and Jacob, the God of our fathers, glorified His Servant Jesus…and His name, through faith in His name, has made this man strong." (Acts 3:12-16)*

The Apostle John, in writing his Gospel, included the miracles of Jesus to convince his readers of Christ's divinity: "*Truly Jesus did many other signs in the presence of His disciples, which are not written in this book; but these are written that you may believe that Jesus is the Christ, the Son of God, and that believing you may have life in His name*" (John 20:30-31). If the miracles of the Bible are just myths and legends, then there is no true Christianity. As the Apostle Paul wrote to the early Christians of the church at Corinth: "*If the dead do not rise, then Christ is not risen. And if Christ is not risen, your faith is futile; you are still dead in your sins*" (1 Corinthians 15:16-17). Christianity rises and falls on the reality of miracles.

But miracles aren't just for Bible times. God does not change—Jesus is the same "*yesterday, today, and forever*" (Hebrews 13:8). The God who did miracles in the Bible is still a miracle-working God. There are countless stories of modern-day miracles. You can read all about some of them by reading the biographies of Christians like George Mueller, Smith Wigglesworth, John G. Lake, and Kathryn Khulman. These examples of modern-day miracles prove that God is real and that He cares for people who put their faith in Him.

What is the difference between Christianity and other religions?

As an evangelist, part of my mission in life is to preach about Jesus to people. I have had the privilege of going all over the world to preach the Gospel. When I preach in Muslim nations and hold up my Bible with its black leather cover and gold-edged pages, the Muslims in the audience hold up a copy of the Koran with a black leather cover and gold-edged pages. What right do I have to say that my book is the truth? The answer: Miracles.

When I preach about Jesus. I tell stories about the miracles Jesus did in the Bible. I tell them, as it says in Hebrews 13:8, that *"Jesus Christ is the same yesterday, today, and forever."* I announce that if Jesus is truly alive, He will perform miracles. Then I pray for the sick in the name of Jesus. After we pray, I invite people who have been healed to come to the platform and testify. Often dozens and sometimes hundreds of people come forward to share they have been healed.

In my ministry I have seen blind eyes opened, deaf ears hearing, and cripples walking. These miracles prove that Jesus is alive today. The Bible says that God confirms the preaching of His word with miraculous signs (Mark 16:20). When I ask people to take the leap of faith and surrender their lives to Jesus, thousands pray with me to receive salvation. Many of them do so because of the miracles they have seen with their own eyes during the service.

The Story of the Ethiopian Mohammad

One time I was preaching in Metu, Ethiopia. Ethiopia is about 30% Muslim and there is a high concentration of Muslims in Metu. The Muslims in Metu were not happy that I was going to be preaching about Jesus in their town. Some Muslim young people followed our team around and tore down the posters that we put up to announce our Gospel festival. At one point, these youth started a riot and threw stones at our team, with one of the stones breaking the windshield of our publicity vehicle. Because of the public disturbance, the police were called in. The Muslims blamed the riot on our team (not that

that made much sense, since it was our own equipment that was being damaged). Seventeen of our team members were thrown into jail, and we had to hire a lawyer to help us get them free. Despite these problems, the festival still went forward.

However, on the first night we were disappointed because not many people attended the service. Since all our posters had been torn down, very few people knew of the festival. After the service, I prayed and asked God to do a miracle. The next night, a crippled man attended the service. This man was well known in the community, as he was always seen hobbling around on a stick and asking people for money. When we prayed for the sick that evening, Jesus touched this crippled man and he suddenly began to walk. He held his crutch up in the air and ran up to the platform to show everyone what had happened. He kept shouting, "Jesus healed me! Jesus healed me!" We asked him, "What is your name?" He replied, "My name is Mohammad." Immediately, everyone in the crowd knew he was a Muslim. Because he was healed, word began to spread that Jesus was healing Muslims. The next night, the crowd size doubled. The following night, it doubled again. By the end of our five-day festival, over fifty-five thousand people were gathered on the field to hear about Jesus. Many of these people were Muslims who wanted to see Jesus do miracles.

Miracles are a vital proof of God's existence

Healing evangelist Reinhard Bonnke believed that some Christians put too much emphasis on logic and not enough emphasis on miracles. He preached:

> The church has too often trusted scholarship, genius, logic, and philosophy. According to 1 Corinthians 1:27, God has chosen the foolish things to confound the wise. The apostles did not preach logic, they preached the power of God. Far too often, Christians become like lawyers in a court. We argue about Jesus to get a positive verdict on Him. This is human wisdom. Jesus needs no defending. You don't need to defend a lion, all you need to do is open his cage. Jesus will be the judge of all the earth. We are not

called to be lawyers or attorneys or barristers, we are called to be witnesses. Jesus said, "You are my witnesses." A witness only tells what he has seen or experienced. He does not give speeches, he does not debate. The witness becomes a living piece of evidence. The living Jesus needs living witnesses. I want to be a living piece of evidence that Jesus is alive.

Bonnke witnessed thousands of miracles during his years of ministry in Africa. The miracles he witnessed made his faith unshakable.

Many apologists emphasize the miracles of Jesus but fail to defend the idea that miracles can happen today. In fact, there is little difference between the attitude of the cessationist (Christians who believe that miracles only happened in Bible times) and that of an atheist with regard to miracles that happen in the present: they both think that miracles do not happen. Cessationists make this mistake to avoid the difficulties of answering questions about why some people do not receive miracles and why some miracle stories appear to be hoaxes. They also want to avoid being lumped in with faith-preachers who they see as flamboyant conmen.

But the argument against miracles is often an argument from a lack of experience. Atheists often say they have never witnessed a genuine miracle. However, once someone experiences a genuine miracle, his or her personal experience is a powerful proof of God's existence. Healing evangelist Mike Francen says, "A miracle settles the issue." Once someone sees a miracle with her own eyes or experiences a miracle in his own body, there is no more argument about the reality of miracles, and by extension of the existence of God. It is difficult for an atheist to talk a believer out of his or her deeply held beliefs when the believer has had significant experiences of God. Personal experience is much stronger evidence then a philosophical argument. As one evangelist said, "A man with an experience is not at the mercy of a man with an argument."

David Hume and the argument against miracles

David Hume (1711-1776), a Scottish philosopher and atheist, believed that miracles were impossible. In 1748, he published an essay "Of Miracles" that argues against their existence. Hume begins his discussion with the presupposition that miracles are impossible since "a miracle is a violation of the laws of nature." By assuming that miracles are impossible, he tried to prove that miracles cannot exist.

Hume rightly observes that the proof for miracles relies upon the testimonies of those who witness them. He writes:

> *…we may observe, that there is no species of reasoning more common, more useful, and even necessary to human life, than that which is derived from the testimony of men, and the reports of eye-witnesses and spectators […] It will be sufficient to observe, that our assurance in any argument of this kind is derived from no other principle than our observation of the veracity of human testimony, and of the usual conformity of facts to the reports of witnesses.*[2]

But when eyewitness accounts of miracles are presented, Hume immediately rejects the credibility of these accounts because "no testimony is sufficient to establish a miracle." The only way a miracle could be proved to have occurred is if "the testimony be of such a kind, that its falsehood would be more miraculous." According to Hume, a person who claimed to have witnessed a miracle was either "deceived or trying to deceive." In other words, for a miracle to be believable, there needed to be a greater chance of the miracle happening than that the person reporting about the miracle was telling a lie. Since Hume had never witnessed a miracle and believed that miracles were impossible, it seemed to him that the greater chance was that those who reported miracles were lying.

For Hume, "barbarous and ignorant peoples" are those who report the most miracles—people who, because they don't have access to science, can be led to believe in the miraculous as the explanation for phenomena they cannot otherwise account for. Miracles, wherever they seemed to have occurred were just hoaxes. Or if they were not hoaxes, they were simply some psychosomatic effect that could be explained by science or by an unexplained natural law that science had not discovered yet.

Hume also argued that miracles could not be used as proof that one religion was more true than another, since, as Hume points out, each religion makes miraculous claims. He writes:

> *Let us consider, that, in matters of religion, whatever is different is contrary [...] Every miracle, therefore, pretended to have been wrought in any of these religions (and all of them abound in miracles) [...] has the same force [...] to overthrow every other system. [...] therefore we may establish it as a maxim, that no human testimony can have such force as to prove a miracle, and make it a just foundation for any system of religion.*[3]

So, where Christians point to the miracles of Jesus as proof for the truth of Christianity, Hindus and Muslims also claim to experience miracles. These competing claims, according to Hume, cancel out miracles as a proof for the claims of different religions.

Hume's essay was much discussed in his own time and continues to receive attention from atheists. Like Hume, modern atheists believe that reports of miracles are lies and that those who believe in the miraculous are either ignorant or have been imposed on. They point out that ancient societies attributed anything they did not understand to magic or to a god. For example, the Norsemen believed that Thor caused lightening because they had not discovered the scientific explanation for lightening. But now that science can explain lightening, no one believes in Thor anymore. As scientific knowledge increases, atheists argue that there is less and less room to believe that God is the explanation for what science has left unexplained.

But the arguments of Hume and the atheists are flawed

1. Hume fails to account for the unusual event. In rejecting miracles, Hume believed that massive amounts of daily experience when miracles do not occur count as far greater evidence against miracles then the occasional report of a miraculous event counted for them. However, his reasoning is flawed because it fails to account for the occasional event that is outside the ordinary. For example, in daily experience, it is exceptional for someone to win the lottery. It is likely true to say that none of us have won the lottery or know anyone who has. Using Hume's reasoning, we would be justified in disbelieving that someone won the lottery because the event is outside the ordinary. The improbability of the experience would be proof enough that the report of someone winning is a lie. But, no matter how unlikely it is for a person to win the lottery, every week someone does win.

Another example of an unusual event would be a person being hit with lightening. It is not often that people are hit by lightning, and people who are hit by lightning don't always survive to tell the tale. But Roy Sullivan, a US Park Ranger was struck by lightning, not once, but seven times over the course of 35 years. To be struck by lightning on average once very 5 years is very unusual. But however unusual, Mr. Sullivan's experiences were documented and have secured him a mention in the Guinness Book of World Records. In the same way, even if it is unusual (based on one's daily experience) for miracles to occur, it is wrong to completely reject every report of miracles just because they are unusual.

2. Hume fails to account for the fact that the God who created the laws of nature can supersede the laws of nature. One cannot argue against miracles by pointing to natural law, because miracles (by definition) are supernatural. If there is an all-powerful God, then it is obvious that He could perform miracles. When God does a miracle, He is not violating the laws of nature, rather He is adding a new element to nature. The law of gravity says that an apple dropped from my hand will be drawn toward the center of the earth, but that fall can be stopped if someone else's hand intercepts the apple. The intervening hand does not violate the law of gravity, it simply adds something new to the equation. In the same way, a miracle does not suspend the laws of nature; it just adds a supernatural dimension to the laws of nature. When God heals a sick man, that man is still subject to the natural process of decay.

3. Hume fails to account for the truth of experiences he has never experienced. Once there were some Dutch traders who visited a king of Siam. The Dutch traders told the king that in their country, the weather got so cold that the rivers froze solid and horses could walk on the ice. The king immediately concluded the traders were lying to him because he had never seen water freeze. By Hume's reasoning, the king was perfectly justified in refusing to believe the traders because the experience they related was one he had never seen for himself. But that the king refused to believe the traders' testimony had no bearing on the fact that, in cold weather, rivers undoubtedly freeze over. Lack of personal experience cannot be proof that an experience had by others is invalid or untrue.

4. Hume's argument is meaningless to the person who experiences a miracle. Ultimately, the proof Hume is wrong are the words of the man in John 19:25, *"One thing I know: that though I was blind, now I see."* No one can take this blind man's testimony away from him. He will forever believe in miracles because he experienced one for himself. The Siamese king would never be able to convince the Dutch traders that water cannot freeze just because he had never seen it happen. They had seen it happen, and their experience would be stronger than an uninformed opinion.

5. Hume failed to accept testimony, no matter how strong the witness. "There is always more reason to disbelieve the report of miracles then to believe the report," concluded Hume. Such a statement is only meaningful if someone has decided already that miracles are impossible. However, the possibility of miracles must not be judged by belief to the contrary, but by the record of historical evidence. Craig S. Keener, a Christian theologian, professor and author, has recorded thousands of modern-day miracles from all parts of the world.[4] I have witnessed God do many miracles in Gospel festivals that I have led. Thousands of Christians over the centuries have experienced miracles.

Can all this testimony be wrong? The argument against miracles is like the old story of the conversation between the atheist philosopher and the Christian. One day the two were arguing about whether miracles really occur. The philosopher brought up the miraculous delivery of the Israelites from Pharaoh as an example:

"Remember the children of Israel who crossed the Red Sea? Well, that was not really a miracle. You see," he explained, "at the point where they crossed the sea, it was shallow. The 'miracle' was that Moses found water that was only one foot deep."

"Only one foot deep!" the Christian exclaimed, "That makes for an even greater miracle."

"What are you talking about?" asked the philosopher.

"Well," the Christian replied, "that means God drowned the entire Egyptian army in only one foot of water."

In the same way, for the sea of testimony in support of miracles to be all wrong, "an even greater miracle" would be required—one that could make those who had been blind believe they always saw, or make those who had been crippled believe they never needed a cane, or make those who had been sick believe that the sickness had just been a state of mind. No matter what anyone else tells me about miracles, the best evidence I have is my own experience of God's supernatural power. And my experience tells me:

God is THERE!

PROOF

CHAPTER 8
Redemptive Proof—Evidence from Religious Experience

Premise A: *People claim to have experienced life-change by encountering God.*

Premise B: *There is no reason for these people to lie about their experience.*

Premise C: *Others bear witness to the miraculous change in these same people.*

Conclusion: *Therefore, a life-changing God exists.*

Every society has believed in the supernatural. Ancient Egyptians worshiped Isis, Ra, Anubis, and Horus. Hindus bow before Shiva, Krishna, Vishnu, Kali, and believe in three hundred million other gods. The Greeks believed in Zeus and the Olympians. The Norsemen served Odin. The Germanic people worshiped Thor, the god of thunder. In many Asian cultures, people worship their ancestors. The Mayans believed in Kukulcan, Chac, Kinich Ahau, and Yum Cimil. Tribal societies in North America and Africa have their native and shamanistic spiritualism. The Jew, the Christian, and the Muslim each have their different creeds. The fact that human history shows a general and persistent belief in supernatural entities is a powerful proof for the existence of the supernatural. The reason humans search for God is because they know He exists.

To defend against the worldwide agreement about belief in the supernatural, Atheists claim that the existence of many different gods is proof that no god exists. Because Christians don't believe in the gods of Hinduism, Islam, or other religions, atheists say, "I just believe in one fewer god than you do. When you understand why you dismiss all the other possible gods, you will understand why I dismiss yours."[1] But saying people are atheists because they don't believe in all gods is like saying everybody is single because no one is married to everybody. Besides, the Ten Commandments clearly allow for the existence of the supernatural outside of God when they say, *"You shall have no other gods before me"* (Exodus 20:3). Christians don't believe that no other gods exist, they simply know they are to put their faith only in the One Supreme God by whom all things exist.

The testimony of the Apostle Paul

There is often a remarkable change when someone becomes a Christian. When people give their lives to Christ, their habits change—people who were compulsive gamblers don't gamble anymore, a husband who abused his wife turns things around, an alcoholic is freed of a desire to drink. Thousands of Christians have testimonies about how their lives have been changed by the power of God. The Apostle Paul explained these stories of transformation: *"Therefore, if anyone is in Christ, he is a new creation; old things have passed away; behold, all things have become new"* (2 Corinthians 5:17).

There is no greater testimony to the life-transforming power of God than the story of Saul of Tarsus who became Paul the Apostle. He was born a Jew and studied under Gamaliel, the greatest rabbi of his time. He was passionate about his Jewish traditions, and, as a result, he fervently hated the new sect of Jesus' followers. He was a witness to the martyrdom of Stephen, holding the cloaks of those who stoned him. He threw Christians—whole families of them—in prison. In his determination to persecute believers, he received permission to travel to Damascus and oppress any Christ-followers there. Saul was a Jew, he was totally committed to his Jewish community, and his status and prospects depended on his love for his Jewish faith and nation.

But on the road to Damascus, he had a surprise encounter with the risen Christ. Jesus appeared and spoke to him in a blinding light that knocked him off his horse. Because of this encounter with Jesus, Saul became a Christian. Initially, other Christians were skeptical about his conversion, but it soon became obvious that he was as passionate about preaching his new faith as he had ever been about persecuting it. As the Apostle Paul, he spent the rest of his life traveling around the Roman Empire and telling people about Jesus. He also wrote over half the books of the New Testament. Saul went from murdering Christians to being one. He went from being a Jew, with all the advantages that conferred on him, to being a follower of Jesus and exposing himself to a life of persecution. He went from someone who hated Jesus to someone who died for his faith in Jesus. The reason he gave for this tremendous change was his encounter with the living God. The same God still changes people's lives today.

How God changed my father's life

My father was accepted to West Point, the elite military academy of the United States. He was a proud man, intellectual and arrogant. He had read lots of philosophy and thought he was one of the five smartest men in the world. He said, "I never met the other four, but I figure I am in the top five." However, two weeks before graduating from the Academy, my father's arrogance got the better of him. He walked into the campus bookstore and saw a jacket that he liked. While he had the money to buy it in his pocket, instead of taking it to the till, he tucked the jacket under his arm and walked out of the store. Two military policemen saw him do this and he was arrested for theft. He told the officers, "I just forgot to pay"—but they didn't believe him. Because of this incident he was not allowed to graduate.

If my father had graduated, he would have entered the military as a second lieutenant. But, because of his mistake, he had to serve as a private. The Army sent him to Germany where he was assigned to be an orderly at a military hospital. There he met a Christian. The man tried to witness to my father, but my father argued vehemently with him. My father thought the Christian was foolish and stupid because he had no answer for my father's philosophical diatribes. But one day, my father realized he was miserable, and the Christian was happy. My father asked himself, "Why am I so miserable while this dumb Christian is always happy?" Being a smart guy, he decided to investigate Christianity.

He began by reading through the entire Bible in four months. He started in Genesis, and by the time he finished the book of Revelation, he realized that he believed what he was reading. He became a Christian, and from that time on his life was completely transformed. His arrogance and pride were broken and he started caring about other people. Some years later, after my father had met and married my mother, he was called into Christian ministry. He remembered that the Christian who had witnessed to him had talked about attending Oral Roberts University, so my father decided to apply to the seminary there. When he arrived on campus, he found the man's apartment and knocked on the door. On opening the door and seeing the proud man who had always argued with him, the Christian tried to slam the door in my father's face. But my father stuck his foot in and exclaimed, "No, you don't understand—I've changed. I'm a Christian now!"

History is proof that Jesus changes lives

The Bible and history record life-changing encounter after life-changing encounter of humans with God. Adam walked with God in the Garden of Eden. Abraham heard God's voice; Moses saw God's face; David experienced God's presence. Peter, James, and John walked the dusty streets of Israel with Jesus, God Incarnate. On December 6, 1273, the medieval theologian Thomas Aquinas, experienced a heavenly vision. Both Saint Augustine and Martin Luther encountered God's grace in the book of Romans. Joan of Arc (1412-1431) had visions from God.

These encounters with God have led people to live lives of sacrifice to spread the Gospel and see people set free. David Brainerd (1718-1747) took the Gospel to the American Indians; William Carrey (1761-1834) became a missionary to India, Hudson Taylor (1832-1905) went to China, and Adoniram Judson ministered in Burma. Jim Elliot gave his life to take the Gospel to the Auca Indians in the Amazon jungle. William Wilberforce, a British politician, worked tirelessly to end the scourge of slavery. A thief before he was saved, George Muller established homes to help thousands of orphaned children. Because of her faith in Christ, Corrie Ten Boom was able to forgive the Nazis who imprisoned her family and tormented her sister (who died in a concentration camp).

John Chrysotom, an early church father, said, "Let us overcome by our manner of living rather than by our words alone. For this is the main battle, this is the unanswerable argument, the argument from conduct." In the course of American history, many men and women have been the living example of this statement. George Whitfield, Jonathan Edwards, Francis Asbury, Charles Finney, D.L. Moody, Billy Sunday, R.A. Torrey, Aimee Semple McPherson, and Billy Graham have all testified to the life-changing power of God. Each of these people dedicated themselves to the proposition that the God of the Bible exists. They preached about Jesus, took care of orphans, opened hospitals, fed the hungry, and defended the faith. They gave their wealth, their energy, and some their lives because they believed in a living God.

Luis Palau, a fellow evangelist, shares a story about an atheist, who, during a debate, proclaimed that atheism had "done more for the world than Christianity." In response, Palau promised to produce one hundred men whose lives have been changed for the better by Christ if the atheist could bring in one hundred men whose lives have been changed for the better by atheism. The atheist was forced to sit down because he knew he would lose the challenge.[2] While Atheists mock the Christian faith by pretending to worship the "Flying Spaghetti Monster" or the "Invisible Pink Unicorn," such ridicule is rendered powerless in the face of clear evidence that people have been transformed by their faith in Christ. When did the Invisible Pink Unicorn ever cure a drug addiction? When did the Flying Spaghetti Monster ever turn a wife-abuser into a loving husband? But the reality that Christianity changes peoples' lives in an instant is beyond dispute.

Ad Populum proof for God's existence

The atheist might say that this accumulation of evidence just proves that people have been deceived for a long time about the existence of God. Claiming that people are deceived about the divine is one of four responses available to people who are presented with the evidence from religious experience:

1. The person may be lying. For personal gain or glory the person has falsely claimed an encounter with the divine.

2. The person may be deceived. They are not lying, but the experience they had was not a legitimate experience of the divine. Rather, it was some trick that they are the dupe of.

3. The person may be misinformed and improperly interpreting the evidence. No one is tricking them, but the experience they had is not really supernatural. Instead, it was a hallucination, or a mirage, or some other kind of unexplained natural phenomenon.

4. The person is telling the truth. They really had an encounter with God.

Given the sheer number of testimonies to the existence of the divine and of lives that have been changed by God, the last of these responses cannot be dismissed. Imagine you are on a jury in a court of law. For the case being tried, you hear the testimony of one witness after another—and the witness of one is only confirmed by the witness of the others. Now, given the possibility that one person may be deceived, and that ten people might be trying to pull off a practical joke, and that hundreds more might be crazy, what are the chances that the testimony of millions and millions of people could all be wrong? In the court of human history and experience, the evidence from the witnesses is overwhelmingly in favor of the existence of God. There are too many witnesses to refute. There are too many who say, "I saw Him!"—"I heard Him!"—"He healed me!"—"I know that He exists!"

Two thousand years of testimonies gives me great confidence in the value of believing, not just in the supernatural in some general way, but in the God of the Bible specifically, and in Jesus Christ His Son. I add my own experiences of God to the tide of that testimony. God has spoken to me. I have seen Him do miracles. He has answered my prayers, not just once or twice, but hundreds of times. As Alfred Ackley, the hymn writer, sings, "You ask me how I know He lives? He lives within my heart!"

God is THERE!

Each one of the seven proofs presented has its flaws and counterarguments, and it could be argued that no one proof is enough to prove conclusively that God exists. But think of these seven proofs as the stones in an arch. No arch is held up by a single stone. The architectural marvel of the arch is in the capacity that all the stones together have of supporting tremendous weight. In the same way, when all these proofs are considered together, they are strong enough to support the weight of proving God's existence. When I consider all the evidence—from cause, from design, from reason, from morals, from the Bible, from miracles, and from experience—I say: God is THERE.

Christianity is not built on blind faith, but on faith supported by strong evidence. The thinking person can embrace the Christian faith on a rational basis. But even with all the evidence, believing in God is still a matter of faith. As William Lane Craig has said: "Pascal was right in maintaining that God has given evidence sufficiently clear for those with an open heart, but sufficiently vague so as not to compel those whose hearts are closed."[3] Having a closed heart to God isn't unnatural in life or abnormal in any way—because of sin, every human is naturally closed-hearted. But the evidence for God IS there, and I encourage you to lay aside disappointment, or weariness, or skepticism, or whatever else may be closing you off. According to Pascal, "Those who seek God find Him."[4] If you will open your heart to the evidence for God, you will find that God is waiting for you. You will discover:

God is THERE!

PART 2:
DOES GOD CARE?

The Kind of God Who Exists

CHAPTER 9
The Problem of Evil

Premise A: *If a good God does not exist, evil also does not exist.*

Premise B: *Evil exists.*

Conclusion: *Therefore, a good God exists.*

The preceding chapters have provided several proofs for the existence of God, but I can understand not being ready to trust in God if all you know about Him is that He exists. I know that my next-door neighbors exist, but that doesn't mean I'm ready to let them take care of my children. Before I let someone do that, I want to know that I can trust them with the most precious things in my life. So, if God exists, the question must be asked: "What sort of God is He?"

With seven billion people on a planet that is part of a star system that is one among billions in the universe, someone might wonder: Is He the sort of God to care about individual people? Does He see my pain and understand my sorrow? Does He know what brings me joy and shake His head at my pet peeves? Does He listen when I pray at night and watch over me as I go about my day? Is He willing to do things to help me when I need help? When I'm sick, or sorrowful, or disappointed, or going through a dark time in life, is God there for me? Will He be waiting for me when I die? Psalms 8:3-4 asks the same questions, *"When I consider Your heavens, the work of Your fingers, the moon and the stars, which You have ordained, What is man that You are mindful of him, and the son of man that You visit him?"* So many questions, and at the core of them, just one question: Does God care about me?

Christians answer this question with a confident, "Yes, God does care!" According to the Bible, God is all-powerful (omnipotent), all-knowing (omniscient), and all-good (omni-benevolent). Christians believe that every good thing that a person experiences can be traced back to God. But human experience proves another truth: evil exists.

It is undeniable that there is evil in this world. There are natural disasters like tornados, earthquakes, hurricanes, tidal waves, and floods. There are physical diseases and conditions like cancer, strokes, Alzheimer's, birth defects, and genetic disorders. There is also evil caused by humans. Some human-caused evil is unintentional, such as pain caused by car wrecks and medical mistakes; other human-caused evil is intentional like theft, murder, slander, and rape. Every human being goes through times of emotional pain and physical suffering. During these times, there is a tendency for people to wonder if God is real and to question if He cares about their problems.

The existence of evil is one of the main objections to the Christian God. A commentator on Reddit asked, "Does it make sense to believe that an all-powerful, infinitely loving, and merciful deity is out there who refuses to stop genocide, cancer, child sexual abuse, and starvation?" Another person wrote, "What causes a little girl to get a tumor in her brain? And don't give me the god-works-in-mysterious-ways copout." George Barna, the Christian pollster, conducted a nationwide survey asking the question, "If you could ask God one question and you knew He would give you an answer, what would you ask? The most popular response—it was proposed by 17% of the respondents—was "Why is there pain and suffering in the world?"[1]

Atheists and the problem of evil

Atheists often use the problem of evil to argue against the existence of God. In his essay "God and Evil," H.J. McCloskey wrote, "Evil is a problem, for the theist, in that a contradiction is involved in the fact of evil on the one hand and belief in the omnipotence and omniscience of God on the other."[2] David Hume phrased the problem this way: "Is God willing to prevent evil, but not able? Then he is not omnipotent. Is he able, but not willing? Then he is malevolent. Is he both able and willing? Then whence cometh evil? Is he neither able nor willing? Then why call him God?"

Various thinkers have tried to resolve this dilemma by denying different characteristics of the God of the Bible. After his son died of a rare and painful disease, Rabbi Harold Kushner, in his book, *When Bad Things Happen to Good People*, denies the validity of God's omnipotence. While God knows about your pain and wants to help you through your pain, Kushner came to believe that God is unable to alleviate your pain.[3] He portrays God as a "kind-hearted wimp." Others have denied the omni-benevolence of God. Alan Carter proposes the possibility of an evil God and suggests that God is not as good as we think He is and that He is just playing a trick on us.[4]

Another way to dodge the problem of evil is to deny that evil exists. This is the approach of some forms of Hinduism, Zen Buddhism, some New Age religions, and mind-science sects like Christian Science. Rather than saying that God is not all-powerful, or all-knowing, or all-good, this approach says that evil is not real because it is just a problem of perception. Good and evil and right and wrong exist in the mind and do not have objective reality.

A final way to reconcile the nature of God with the existence of evil is to demonstrate that it is possible for God to be all-powerful, all-knowing, and all-good and for evil to exist at the same time. This is the Christian understanding of the dilemma.

A Christian understanding of evil

In the Christian worldview, God is good, and He created everything to be good. *"God saw everything that He had made, and indeed it was very good"* (Genesis 1:31). God is not the author of evil, rather evil is simply a corruption of God's perfect plan. Saint Augustine, one of the Early Church Fathers, argued that evil is a lack of good. Nothing is evil in itself; it is simply the absence of what is good. Good is normal, evil is an abnormality. For example, cancer is caused by cells that misbehave. Rape is a perversion of a normal, good, God-created impulse to procreate. God made everything to be good, and it only becomes bad when it is misused or corrupted. God made gravity, and it is good—it keeps us on planet earth and keeps planet earth in its orbit. But when someone falls into the Grand Canyon, as happens almost every year, the goodness of gravity certainly seems evil.

All evil in the world can be traced back to sin. Sin is an abnormality. When God created the world, He gave humans dominion over all of creation (Genesis 1:28). But, Adam and Eve, the first man and woman, brought sin into the world. They did this by disobeying God, who, after giving them the whole world, told them of only one thing they were not to do: *"Of the tree of the knowledge of good and evil you shall not eat"* (Genesis 2:17). Adam and Eve chose to disobey God, and it was through them that sin entered the world. With sin came death, disease, and natural tragedy. Sin corrupted God's perfect creation.

There are two categories of evil: general evil and specific evil. General evil is the result of general sin. When Adam and Eve sinned, they introduced a foreign abnormal element into God's perfectly functioning universe. It was like throwing sand into the gas tank of a car: the car might continue to run for a while, but eventually the gears will start to grind and the car engine will come to a halt. In the same way, since sin was introduced into the world, the world continues to run but now there are problems like earthquakes, tornados, hurricanes, and species that are going extinct. Romans 8:20-22 explains,

> *For the creation was subjected to frustration, not by its own choice, but by the will of the one who subjected it, in hope that the creation itself will be liberated from its bondage to decay and brought into the freedom and glory of the children of God. We know that the whole creation has been groaning as in the pains of childbirth right up to the present time.*

Paul's idea of creation groaning is like the sound of sand grinding in the gears of a car. When we look at creation, it is obvious there are imperfections. Earthquakes, tornados, and hurricanes cause enormous destruction. Because of sin, the further we get from the moment of Creation, the more grinding we see and hear in the world. In fact, Jesus taught that in the last days we would see increased war, pestilence, famine, and earthquakes (Matthew 24:11).

The second category of evil, specific evil, is caused by specific sinful actions of specific sinful individuals. Often poverty is caused by people making poor choices—some people are greedy and grasp at too much; other people act foolishly and end up in want. Obesity is caused by eating too much food—an example of the sin of gluttony. Car wrecks are often caused by someone breaking the law by choosing to speed. War can be caused by greed, hate, and pride. On 9/11 when two planes flew into the World Trade Center, the loss of thousands of lives was the result of the evil choices of the hijackers.

Free will is the reason evil exists

God did not cause Adam and Eve to sin. He simply allowed them to have *free choice* which led to sin. Adam and Eve sinned of their own free will. For free will to exist, choice must also be allowed to exist. The choice that Adam and Eve were given was the choice to obey God or to disobey God. Adam and Eve needed to have the option of disobeying God or they would not have been truly free. The exercise of their freedom to choose brought sin, pain, suffering, and death into the world. God knew He was taking a risk by making humans free; but, if He didn't make us free, we would also not be human.

The existence of free-will makes evil necessary. Alvin Plantinga wrote,

> *A world containing creatures who are significantly free (and freely perform more good than evil actions) is more valuable, all else being equal, than a world containing no free creatures at all. Now God can create free creatures, but He can't cause or determine them to do only what is right. For if He does so, then they aren't*

significantly free after all; they do not do what is right freely. To create creatures capable of moral good, therefore, He must create creatures capable of moral evil; and He can't give these creatures the freedom to perform evil and at the same time prevent them from doing so. As it turned out, sadly enough, some of the free creatures God created went wrong in the exercise of their freedom; this is the source of moral evil. The fact that free creatures sometimes go wrong, however, counts neither against God's omnipotence nor against His goodness; for He could have forestalled the occurrence of moral evil only by removing the possibility of moral good.[5]

A world without the possibility of evil, is a world without free will. A world where free will exists, means the option to choose between something that will have good consequences and something that will have evil consequences. It is a tragedy when people choose evil, but the good of free will outweighs the tragedy of evil.

We all agree that it is a tragedy when a drunk driver hits another car, killing its innocent passengers. We could stop the evil of drunkenness and its consequences from ever happening by outlawing all drinking of alcohol. The United States tried this during Prohibition but gave up the experiment after thirteen years of chasing down bootleggers and moonshiners who illegally provided alcohol to the thirsty public. Perhaps if America had adopted the policy that Singapore has of dealing with drug dealers (executing them) Prohibition would have been more successful. Executing someone for getting drunk would likely go a long way to preventing drunk driving from ever killing another man, woman, or child. But, as a society, we have decided that it is better for people to have the freedom to drink than it is to stop the evil of drunk driving and its sometimes terrible consequences.

God made a similar decision in creating humanity. He decided it is more important for humans to have free will than it is to stop evil from existing. He has the power to stop all evil from occurring, but to do so, He would have to remove our free will. God could have created people to be robots, programming them never to do anything evil. But a robot has no free choice and experiences no rewards for doing what it is programed to do. When a robot puts a screw in a car, the robot does not earn wages from the company. It is simply doing what it is programed to do. Human robots who did the good they were programmed to do, would not feel rewarded by doing good. C. S. Lewis wrote,

> Why, then, did God give [people] free will? Because free will, though it makes evil possible, is also the only thing that makes possible any love or goodness or joy worth having. A world of automata— of creatures that worked like machines—would hardly be worth creating. The happiness which God designs for His higher creatures is the happiness of being freely, voluntarily united to Him and to each other [...]. And for that, they must be free. Of course, God knew what would happen if they used their freedom the wrong way: apparently He thought it worth the risk.[6]

Some might say that God could create a world with both free will and an absence of evil, but this is logically impossible. God can do anything, but God cannot do what is logically impossible to do. It would be like creating a square circle or declaring that 2+2=5. Creating a world with both free choice and no consequences from making bad decisions is impossible. So, God chose the best possible option which involved giving humans free choice, even though He knew this free choice could and would lead to sin, pain, suffering and all sorts of evil.

Evil proves that a good God exists

While the existence of evil is a serious problem, it is an even more serious problem for atheists because the existence of evil is only further evidence for God's existence. For atheists, evil is a problem because their worldview doesn't really allow it to exist. They don't believe in God and they certainly do not believe in the devil. As one militant online atheist typed, "I don't believe in your sky daddy or your hole hobbit." But without God, the terms "good" and "evil" in the mouth of an atheist are subjective, relative terms, not moral absolutes. For the atheist, there is only personal good, or societal good, or an action that is good for the species; but there is no objective foundation or standard for concepts of good and evil. Norman Geisler wrote, "Atheism cannot rationally offer a definition of evil without appealing to an ultimate standard of good." C.S. Lewis wrote, "My argument against God was this universe seemed so cruel and unjust. But how had I got this idea of just and unjust? A man does not call a line crooked unless he has some idea of a straight line. What was I comparing this universe with when I called it unjust?"[7]

Like Lewis, atheists know that good and evil exist; but they are not honest about what makes something good or evil. They point to evils—like the Crusades, the Inquisition, and the Salem Witch Trials—and pronounce a judgement of "guilty" upon "evil" Christians. Now, I acknowledge that Christians have made many terrible mistakes in the past, but I dispute the honesty of atheists to judge them. Lewis was an honest atheist who realized that evil, rather than being a problem for God's existence, actually proved that a good God is there.

God's response to suffering

The good news is that God does not leave the people He created alone in the midst of pain and suffering. God is the answer to the problem of evil. The existence of evil should not turn us away from God; instead, it should make us turn toward Him. And it should do so for several reasons.

Firstly, God is the greatest victim of evil. Even though enduring suffering is terrible, God chose to experience it Himself. God came and experienced our suffering with us when Jesus came to earth. Dorothy Sayers wrote:

> For whatever reason God chose to make man as he is—limited and suffering and subject to sorrows and death—He had the honesty and courage to take His own medicine [...]. He has Himself gone through the whole of human experience, from the trivial irritations of family life and the cramping restrictions of hard work and lack of money to the worst horrors of pain and humiliation, defeat, despair, and death. When He was a man, He played the man.

He was born in poverty and died in disgrace, and thought it well worthwhile.[8]

God does not prevent suffering, but He is with people and for people in their suffering.

Secondly, since God has given humans free choice, it becomes our responsibility to stop evil in this world. One day, I became upset with God and shook my fist at Him and said, "The world needs You. Can't You see the hurting, the dying, the poor, and the lost? The world needs You!" God spoke back to me in a quiet whisper, "Daniel, the world needs you." Part of God's answer to the pain in this world is for people to help alleviate that pain. That's why I'm an evangelist, and why my ministry has given away 270,000 meals to the children of Belize, dug water wells for villages in India, and works to convince people to live their lives by faith in Jesus. By living godly lives, we can cure some of the evil in this world.

Thirdly, while we may not be able to solve all evils in this life, the problem of evil will be solved completely in the next life. God's viewpoint is eternal; to Him, evil is but a small blip on the timeline of forever. Evil may be a problem for us, but evil is not a problem for God, because He knows the ultimate end of evil and the sad end of every evil doer: *"For we must all appear before the judgment seat of Christ, so that each of us may receive what is due us for the things done while in the body, whether good or bad"* (2 Corinthians 5:10 NIV).

Finally, God will ultimately bring good out of every situation. Romans 8:28 says, *"All things work together for good to those who love God, to those who are the called according to His purpose."* Even as we suffer, God is working to bring about ultimate good. Ecclesiastes 3:11 says, *"[God] has made everything beautiful in its time. He has also set eternity in the human heart; yet no one can fathom what God has done from beginning to end."* From our finite position it might be difficult to see all the good that God is doing, but the truth is that God is at work, and He knows how to turn our suffering into rejoicing.

Yes, God cares!

Christians know that a good God exists. Christians aren't Christians because they are good, they are Christians because they are honest about the existence of evil. Evil will continue to grip the heart of humankind until we have an encounter with God's goodness. Popular culture wrongly claims that people are basically good. Christians, however, acknowledge the truth: God is good and sinful people are desperately in need of Him to save them from the terrible consequences of their endlessly selfish choices.

Consider this: If God did not care for people, He would not save them. God saves people from sin through His Son, Jesus Christ who died on the cross. Therefore:

God CARES!

CHAPTER 10
Jesus is Proof that God Cares

Premise A: *If God cared for people, He would use His power to help them.*

Premise B: *Jesus, the God-man, healed the sick, loved the outcast, died to save sinners, and rose from the dead to give them eternal life.*

Conclusion: *Therefore, God cares for people.*

Some philosophical ideas of God do not offer much comfort to those who are hurting. One idea is that God is an abstract concept, an impersonal and distant force. This force created the universe, but it neither knows your name nor cares whether you live or die. This concept of God is called Deism. The Deistic worldview sees God as a clockmaker who built a clock, started it ticking, and then left it to run on its own laws and mechanisms. The God of the Deists simply programs the universe. He orchestrates the Big Bang, gives an initial nudge to the evolutionary process, and then steps back and disinterestedly watches the results. This deistic God never reaches into the universe He set going to interfere or intervene.

Others picture God as an elderly figure sitting on a throne way up in heaven. He is "the man upstairs." They think He peeks through the clouds at His creatures far below and the distance is so great that people look like little ants scurrying around. It is hard to imagine the figure on the throne caring about what happens to any individual ant.

But the New Testament offers us a different picture of God. In the four Gospels, we discover Jesus, and His life proves that God cares for us. Jesus is not just a messenger from heaven. He is far more than an angelic being. Jesus is God, and as God, He came from heaven to earth to help us in our suffering. One of the most well-known verses in the Bible says, *"For God so loved the world that He gave His only begotten Son, that whoever believes in Him should not perish but have everlasting life"* (John 3:16). The story of how God became a human is the greatest love story ever told. Let's take a few moments to look at the story of Jesus. The evidence for how much God cares for people is found in the life of Jesus.

The birth of Jesus is proof that God cares

Christianity is rooted in space and time; its claims about Jesus are historical. Two thousand years ago, God Almighty humbled Himself and became a human. He was born to a virgin named Mary in the town of Bethlehem, a few miles from the city of Jerusalem. The King of the Universe was born in a stable and spent His first night on earth with the eating trough of animals as His cradle. Sometimes, when a child leaves the front door of the house open, you will hear the parents say, "You'd think you were born in a barn." Well, that's exactly how Jesus was born. God did not arrive on earth riding in a golden chariot. He did not appear surrounded by ten million angels. No, Jesus was born as a helpless baby. He experienced the trauma of passing through the birthing canal. When He caught His first breath, the "silent night" was disturbed as He wailed like any other human child. C.S. Lewis wrote, "The central miracle asserted by Christians is the Incarnation. They say God became Man."[1]

The reason God did this was not because He was curious about what it would be like to be a man. He did this so that we could understand who He is and how much He cares. Imagine that you wanted to communicate with an ant. As a human, you could talk to an ant, pick it up from the ground, cuddle it, blow on it, write it a long letter, sing it a song, paint it a picture—but the ant would not understand your attempts to communicate. The only way to really get an ant's attention is to become an ant and speak to it in terms it could understand. In a sense, this is what God did for us. In order to reach humans in their pain and brokenness, their great Creator became a man. He walked on the earth, ate our food, shared our sorrows, experienced our pain, and shared a message from heaven with us.

Christians have believed in the virgin birth from the earliest times. The Apostle's Creed, which goes back in its earliest form to the second century, reads:

> *I believe in God the Father Almighty, maker of heaven and earth;*
> *And in Jesus Christ His only Son our Lord:*
> *Who was conceived by the Holy Spirit, born of the Virgin Mary.*

Many of the arguments for God's existence are abstract and philosophical, but in the person of Jesus, God concretely entered human history and revealed Himself to humanity. Jesus shows that God is not an abstract concept, He is a concrete reality. The Gospel of John explains this mystery, *"In the beginning was the Word, and the Word was with God, and the Word was God [...] And the Word became flesh and dwelt among us, and we beheld His glory, the glory as of the only begotten of the Father, full of grace and truth"* (John 1:1,14). When I hear about Jesus leaving the heavenly streets of gold to come walk the dusty roads of Judea with humanity, I say, "Yes, God CARES!"

The life of Jesus is proof that God cares

Jesus grew up, spending His infancy in Bethlehem and Egypt, and then as a child moved to the small town of Nazareth. He learned how to walk and how to talk. Like other boys, He fell and skinned His knee and went running to His mother for comfort. He experienced the joys and the frustrations of childhood. He went to the synagogue and learned about the God of Abraham, Isaac, and Jacob. He heard stories about the life of Moses and King David. He studied the writings of the prophets. *"Jesus increased in wisdom and stature, and in favor with God and men"* (Luke 2:52). As He entered puberty, Jesus amazed the greatest scholars of the Jewish religion with His wisdom.

When He was about thirty years old, Jesus was baptized by His cousin, John. He then went out into the desert wilderness and was tempted by Satan. He experienced the same temptations that every human is offered, but unlike Adam and Eve and the rest of us, He did not give into the temptation to disobey God and live selfishly. When He returned from this place of temptation, He started to preach the Gospel—the Good News that God loves and cares for people and is ready to help them. Calling twelve disciples to follow Him—common men: fishermen, tradesmen, a tax collector—He taught them through simple parables about the Kingdom of God. Besides these twelve, hundreds and thousands would come to hear His words. His teaching transformed their lives. He spoke with great authority and His words captivated His listeners.

One day, young children came to Jesus. The disciples pushed the children away and told them that Jesus was far too important to spend time with them. Jesus saw what they did and was greatly displeased. He said to them, *"Let the little children come to Me, and do not forbid them; for of such is the kingdom of God"* (Mark 10:14). Throughout His ministry, the people that Jewish society thought unimportant— the sick, the poor, women, children, non-Jews, money-grubbing tax collectors, the uneducated—were the people that Jesus would seek out and show God's love to.

The miracles of Jesus are proof that God cares

But Jesus was far more than a traveling teacher. He also performed outstanding miracles and these miracles prove that God cares about people and their circumstances. One day, a leper came to Jesus.

Leprosy was a terrible disease that left people horribly disfigured. It was incurable and was considered contagious because, in Jewish culture, it made a person ritually "unclean." No one wanted to touch a leper because they would become "unclean" too. This leper asked himself a question: "Is Jesus willing to heal me?" Jesus responded to this man's need in a beautiful fashion. Jesus reached out His hand and touched the man, saying, "I am willing. Be healed." Immediately, the man was cured of his leprosy.

Another time, a paralyzed man was carried to Jesus by four friends. Jesus was teaching in a house and the four friends tried to push their way through the crowd that was there listening to Jesus. The crowd was too thick, and it proved impossible to get into the house. In desperation, they carried the paralyzed man up to the roof of the house and dug a hole in it. They then lowered him down through the hole to where Jesus was. Their determination paid off. Jesus spoke kindly to the suffering man, forgave his sins, and healed him.

A woman who was bleeding for twelve years came up behind Jesus in a crowd and touched the edge of His clothes. Immediately she was healed. Jesus raised a man's twelve-year-old daughter from the dead when He touched her hand. He opened a blind man's eyes. He healed a crippled man. Jesus healed a man who could not speak. He healed Peter's mother-in-law from a fever. He changed water into wine, so the guests could continue celebrating. He fed over 5,000 people with five loaves of bread and two small fish. He cast demons out of many people who were possessed by the devil. He raised His dear friend Lazarus from the dead. Sometimes people brought crowds of the sick to Jesus, and scripture tells us that Jesus healed them all (Matthew 15:30).

The Bible records miracle after miracle of Jesus. These miracles prove two things. First, they prove that Jesus is God. Man cannot do miracles, but God can. Second, they prove that God cares for people. Jesus cared about the plight of the sick. One time a man prayed, "Dear God, I pray that I could meet Jesus." At his feet lay an open Bible. As the man began to read the four Gospels, he saw Jesus and by seeing Jesus, he met God. The Bible reveals Jesus to us. Jesus shows us what God is like. The Bible clearly shows us that Jesus is loving, that He heals the sick, that He is compassionate, that He seeks and saves the lost, and that He is wise and full of life. When I read about how Jesus healed the blind man, restored the crippled man, forgave the prostitute, and played with the children, I say, "Yes, God CARES!"

The death of Jesus is proof that God cares

Jesus came to earth to accomplish more than teaching His disciples about heaven and performing miracles. Jesus was a moral teacher and a wonder-worker only because these roles were part of His larger mission in coming to earth. Jesus came to earth to save humans from their sins. As covered in the previous chapter, in the beginning of time, Adam and Eve sinned. They disobeyed God's commands. All of Adam and Eve's offspring, the whole human race, became sinners as a result. The Bible teaches, *"All have sinned and fall short of the glory of God"* (Romans 3:23). And sin has a terrible price: *"For the wages of sin is death"* (Romans 6:23).

When the Bible says that God is holy, it means He is different from humans because He is without sin. Sin is the opposite of God, and He cannot tolerate it. It might be more correct to say that sin cannot tolerate God, in the same way that bacteria cannot tolerate boiling water. Sin, and all the evil it unleashes, is offensive to God's holy nature. Because of this, it is impossible for sinful humans to have a relationship with God or to enter heaven. Anyone who sins is lost and will spend eternity separated from God who is the source of life and goodness. The Bible calls this eternal destination hell, and to spend the eternity that follows this life separated from God is what it calls "the second death." Jesus came to save us from sin and its terrible penalty.

That's why Jesus gave His life on the cross. Jesus did not deserve to die. He lived a perfect life, a life free from sin. He was completely innocent. But evil men condemned Him to death and nailed Him to a wooden cross. The cross is the ultimate example of God's power to take something evil and turn it for good. Jesus allowed Himself to be put to death so that He could die in our place. In the Old Testament, when someone sinned, they were required to bring a goat or a lamb to the Jewish temple, where it was killed and sacrificed. The innocent animal died in the place of the guilty person who had sinned. Each time they sinned, they had to bring another sacrifice. When Jesus died on the cross, He became a sacrifice for the sins of the whole world.

Today, crosses are made of stone, wood, marble, steel, plastic, and stained glass. Churches put them on top of their buildings, in their foyers, behind the pulpit, and etched into every pew. Believers wear them around their necks and put them on their bumper stickers. But the cross is far more than a decoration. *"And when they had come to the place called Calvary, there they crucified Him"* (Luke 23:33).

Crucifixion was a cruel punishment devised by the Romans. Cicero, a Roman statesman, wrote of crucifixion: "It was the most cruel and shameful of all punishments. Let it never come near the body of a Roman citizen." The eighth amendment to the Constitution of the United States guarantees "no cruel and unusual punishment." Because of this, our society does not allow torture or a painful death penalty. Our prisoners watch TV, study for degrees, and have recreation time. But the Roman Empire had none of our modern protections for criminals. In times past, governments used firing squads, electric chairs, and the hangman's noose. Today, we execute criminals with lethal injection. Arguably the worst means of execution ever conceived was the cross.

To say that crucifixion of Jesus was humiliating and painful would be an understatement. Before He was crucified, Jesus was horribly beaten. The flesh on His back was ripped to shreds with thirty-nine lashes of a leather whip laced with sharp bits of metal and glass. The Roman solders ripped His beard out. To insult Him, a branch of thorns was fashioned into a rough crown and jammed down on His forehead. Soldiers beat Jesus with their fists. When they took Him to be crucified, they forced Jesus to carry the heavy cross. At Calvary, Jesus was stretched out on its rough wooden beams and large nails were hammered through His hands and through His feet. When the cross was raised upright, the pain became excruciating as His raw back grated against the splintered surface in His struggle to breath. In physical agony for hours, Jesus hung naked on the cross, suffering the shame and humiliation of a criminal's death.

When I realize that Jesus died on a cross to pay for my sins, I say, "Yes, God CARES!"

The resurrection of Jesus is proof that God cares

Jesus did not stay dead. After three days, He rose from the dead, and today Jesus is alive! There was nothing special about dying on the cross. The Romans crucified thousands of criminals every year. But coming back from the dead is something special. Everyone dies. Nobody comes back. It was the resurrection of Jesus that caught the religious leaders of Jerusalem off guard. They thought that killing Jesus would solve their problem with Him forever. They thought His disciples would run back to Galilee and His message about the kingdom of God would die with Him. But then He rose from the dead.

According to the Apostle Paul, Christianity rises and falls on the resurrection of Christ *"And if Christ has not been raised, our preaching is useless and so is your faith"* (1 Corinthians 15:14). The cross without the resurrection is impotent and meaningless. If Jesus is still dead, His followers might as well keep their money and lock the church doors on their way home. However, if Jesus died and rose again three days later, then the Bible is true.

The death of Jesus was awful, but His resurrection was amazing. Jesus was buried, but today His tomb is empty. His tomb is the only attraction in the world where people line up to see nothing. I have been to the tomb and crawled around inside and there is nothing there. Jesus is risen! When I see the empty tomb in Israel, when I hear about how God breathed life back into Jesus, when I experience His presence in my life today, I say,

"Yes, God CARES!"

CHAPTER 11
The Existence of Jesus

Premise A: *If Jesus existed, there would be historical records to support his existence.*

Premise B: *The Gospels and other historical records of Jesus' life exist.*

Conclusion: *Therefore, Jesus existed.*

Was Jesus a real person? Did He really live in Israel approximately two thousand years ago? How do we know what Jesus really said and did? Lee Strobel was an investigative journalist before he became a Christian. Instead of looking for scientific proof of God's existence, he decided to approach the question of Jesus' existence the same way an investigative journalist approaches a news story. His search was for legal proof that could establish a case "beyond a reasonable doubt." In *The Case for Christ,*[1] he interviews top scholars concerning historical proof for the claims of Christ.

Strobel asks, "How do we know anything about the past?" How do we know that George Washington crossed the Delaware, or that Plato really lived? None of us were alive back then. Our knowledge of history must rely upon historical reports. In the case of Washington and Plato, we rely on writings that tell us about their lives. Even though we never saw them ourselves, we can judge the reliability of eyewitness reports about them. Scholars believe Washington existed because they believe the reports that were written about his life.

In the case of Jesus, we have four different reports that have been written about His life by people who were eyewitnesses or who interviewed eyewitnesses about His life. These four reports are known as the Gospels of Matthew, Mark, Luke, and John. In addition to the Gospels, there are a variety of other historical reports that prove beyond a reasonable doubt that Jesus really existed. Let's look at some of the evidence.

The Epistles prove that Jesus existed

The Apostle Paul wrote the Epistle to the Galatians in approximately 50 AD. In this book, written twenty years after Jesus ascended to heaven, he confirms that Jesus lived, died, and rose again. In his first letter to the Corinthians believers, Paul states:

> *For I delivered to you first of all that which I also received: that Christ died for our sins according to the Scriptures, and that He was buried, and that He rose again the third day according to the Scriptures, and that He was seen by Cephas, then by the twelve. After that He was seen by over five hundred brethren at once, of whom the greater part remain to the present, but some have fallen asleep. After that He was seen by James, then by all the apostles. Then last of all He was seen by me also, as by one born out of due time.* (1 Corinthians 15:3-8)

When Paul says that most of the 500 people who saw Jesus after the resurrection were still alive, he means they can be called on to corroborate his testimony. Galatians, 1 Corinthians, and other New Testament epistles give evidence of a community of Christians who believed in the physical resurrection of Jesus Christ during the mid-first century.

The four Gospels prove Jesus existed

Gospel simply means good news, and that's what the four Gospels give us—the good news about Jesus the Son of God and Savior of mankind. Matthew, Mark, and Luke are known as the synoptic Gospels because they contain much of the same material. This material (known by scholars as the Q material), may have come directly from the pen of someone who wrote down Jesus' words as he spoke them. Perhaps Matthew, a well-educated tax collector, kept a notebook of Jesus' sayings. The Gospel of John was written by "the disciple whom Jesus loved." John personally walked and talked with Jesus. He saw the miracles he records with his own eyes.

Each of the Gospel writers provides a valuable and slightly different perspective. Matthew writes to a Jewish audience, Mark writes to people living in Rome, Luke writes his Gospel to the Gentiles, and John writes to the Church. Because they are writing to different audiences, the Gospel writers emphasize different aspects of the ministry of Jesus. Matthew focuses on Jesus as the long-awaited king, Mark presents Jesus as a suffering servant, Luke emphasizes the humanity of Jesus, and John reveals the divinity of Jesus.

Much ado has been made about so-called "inconsistencies" between the different Gospel accounts. But, the differences in the stories of the Gospel writers are not a weakness; instead they are strengths. Each of the Gospel writers had a different perspective, just as different witnesses at a car wreck remember different details of what they witnessed. David Limbaugh writes, "These variations are not contradictions. In fact, they add weight to the authenticity of the writings, since if the writers aimed to produce fully synchronized narratives, they could have colluded to vet any discrepancies."[2]

Some have argued that one cannot accept the Gospels as evidence for the life of Jesus because they were written by Christians—the idea being that only non-Christians could be trusted to tell the objective truth about Jesus. But this line of argument is like only trusting books on BBQ that are written by vegans. Often the best proof can be found in the writings of those who have been most impacted by an event. After carefully examining the evidence of the four accounts about the life of Jesus, it can be said with great certainty that Jesus really lived, preached, performed miracles, died, and rose from the dead.

Non-Christian writers prove that Jesus existed

Evidence for the life of Jesus is not just found in the Gospels. He is mentioned by a variety of non-Christian writers in the years following His death.

1. Josephus, a first century Jewish historian, mentions Jesus twice in his *Antiquities of the Jews*. The first time he mentions Christ is when he writes about the condemnation of James, *"the brother of Jesus the so-called Christ."* Later[3] he writes:

> *At this time there was a wise man who was called Jesus. And his conduct was good and he was known to be virtuous. And many people from among the Jews and from the other nations became his disciples. Pilate condemned him to be crucified and to die. And those who became his disciples did not abandon his discipleship. They reported that he had appeared to them three days after his crucifixion and that he was alive.*[4]

Some scholars think part of this statement might be an interpolation by a later Christian editor, but the fact that a Jewish historian mentions Jesus at all is significant.

2. Pliny the Younger wrote to Emperor Trajan around AD 112 seeking advice concerning the prosecution of Christians in the court of law. Concerning Christians, he writes,

> *They were in the habit of meeting on a certain fixed day before it was light, when they sang in alternate verses a hymn to Christ, as to a god, and bound themselves by a solemn oath, not to any wicked deeds, but never to commit any fraud, theft or adultery, never to falsify their word, nor deny a trust when they should be*

called upon to deliver it up; after which it was their custom to separate, and then reassemble to partake of food—but food of an ordinary and innocent kind..⁵

3. The Roman historian Tacitus, writing in 115 AD about the fire that destroyed Rome in AD 64, records:

Nero fastened the guilt [...] on a class hated for their abominations, called Christians by the populace. Christus, from whom the name had its origin, suffered the extreme penalty during the reign of Tiberius at the hands of one of our Procurators Pontius Pilatus, and a most mischievous superstition, thus checked for the moment, again broke out not only in Judaea, the first source of the evil, but even in Rome...⁶

4. In 115 AD, Suetonius wrote about Claudius who was emperor from 41-54 AD. He mentions how a group of Jews were deported from Rome during his reign after disturbances "on the instigation of Chrestus." It is likely that he misspelled Christus. If so, this reference puts Christians living in Rome in the 50's AD.⁷

5. The Babylonian Talmud mentions Jesus in a negative light. In writings dated to AD 70-200, they say, "On the eve of the Passover Yeshu was hanged. For forty days before the execution took place, a herald [...] cried, 'He is going forth to be stoned because he has practiced sorcery and enticed Israel to apostasy'."⁸

6. Lucian of Samosata, a second century Greek satirist, wrote about the early believers:

The Christians [...] worship a man to this day—the distinguished personage who introduced their novel rites, and was crucified on that account [...]. [It] was impressed on them by their original lawgiver that they are all brothers, from the moment that they are converted, and deny the gods of Greece, and worship the crucified sage, and live after his laws.⁹

Yes, Jesus was there

The enormous amount of written accounts of Jesus' existence penned just a few decades after His earthly life provide overwhelming evidence that He really existed. Few historians question the existence of Hannibal, the famous Carthaginian general of the Second Punic War, yet the earliest account we have of him was written by Polybius about one hundred years after the war was over. Most of what we know about Hannibal comes from another historian, Livy, writing more than two hundred years after the fact. The evidence for the life of Buddha in the Pāli Canon was written down about five hundred years after he was alive. But no one disputes the existence of Buddha or the main events of his life. Compared to the historical record supporting Hannibal and Buddha, the written evidence for the existence of Jesus and the events of His life could be considered "hot-off-the-press." Based on this evidence, it is certain that Jesus was a real person.

But what about His claims to be Christ, the Son of God? If they are true, then they prove that God CARES!

CHAPTER 12
The Deity of Jesus

Premise A: *Jesus claimed to be God.*

Premise B: *Jesus is either a liar, a lunatic, or He is what He claimed to be: God.*

Premise C: *Jesus is not a liar or a lunatic.*

Conclusion: *Therefore, Jesus is God.*

No one in all of history has had as much impact as Jesus. Napoleon, the conqueror of Europe, said, "I know men and I tell you that Jesus Christ is no mere man. Between Him and every other person in the world there is no possible term of comparison. Alexander, Caesar, Charlemagne, and I have founded empires. But on what did we rest the creations of our genius? Upon force. Jesus Christ founded His empire upon love; and at this hour millions of men would die for Him."

H.G. Wells, the original science-fiction writer and historian, said, "I am a historian, I am not a believer, but I must confess as a historian that this penniless preacher from Nazareth is irrevocably the very center of history. Jesus Christ is easily the most dominant figure in all history."

Historian Kenneth Scott Latourette wrote, "As the centuries pass, the evidence is accumulating that, measured by His effect on history, Jesus is the most influential life ever lived on this planet."

Philip Schaff observed, "Jesus of Nazareth, without money and arms, conquered more millions than Alexander the Great, Caesar, Mohammed, and Napoleon; without science and learning, He shed more light on things human and divine than all philosophers and scholars combined; without the eloquence of school, He spoke such words of life as were never spoken before or since, and produced effects which lie beyond the reach of orator or poet; without writing a single line, He set more pens in motion, and furnished themes for more sermons, orations, discussions, learned volumes, works of art, and songs of praise than the whole army of great men of ancient and modern times."

J.B. Phillips said this about Jesus, "God may thunder His commands from Mount Sinai and men may fear, yet remain at heart exactly as they were before. But let a man once see his God down in the arena as a Man--suffering, tempted, sweating, and agonized, finally dying a criminal's death--and he is a hard man indeed who is untouched."

Famous and influential people have acknowledged Jesus as the most famous and influential man in history, but the truth is that Jesus claimed to be far more than a man. He claimed to be God. Let's consider His claim to divinity.

Did Jesus claim to be God?

In a Hindu context, it would not be notable for someone to claim to be a god because the Hindus have millions of gods in their pantheon. Likewise, the Greeks and the Romans worshiped many different gods, and the Roman emperors were worshiped as deities. But Jesus was a Jew, and He spoke in the context of a Jewish culture. The foundation of the Jewish religion is monotheism: *"Hear, O Israel, the Lord our God, the Lord is one"* (Deuteronomy 6:4). Jews worshipped only one God. So, for Jesus to claim to be God was extraordinary. His claim instantly subjected Him to the closet scrutiny of the Jewish religious leaders. Did He in fact claim to be God?

1. Jesus used God's name to speak of Himself. When Moses saw God in a burning bush, he asked, "Who are you?" God answered, *"I AM* *who I AM."* Jesus used the same terminology when He said, *"Before Abraham was, I am"* (John 8:58).

He also said, *"I am the resurrection and the life; he who believes in me, though he is dead, yet shall he live"* (John 11:25), *"I am the light of the world"* (John 8:12), *"I am the way, the truth, and the life"* (John 14:6), *"I am the living bread"* (John 6:51), *"I am the door"* (John 10:9), *"I am the Good Shepherd"* (John 10:11), *"I am the true vine"* (John 15:1), and *"I am the Alpha and Omega"* (Revelation 1:7-8).

In using this terminology, it was clear to His listeners that He was equating Himself with Yahwah, God, as He revealed Himself in the Old Testament. To His Jewish listeners, this was blasphemy. For Jesus to call Himself "I AM," was the ultimate in hubris. The use of God's name to describe Himself is proof that Jesus considered Himself to be God.

2. Jesus called Himself the "Son of Man." Eighty times throughout the Gospels, Jesus refers to Himself as "the Son of Man." When casual Bible readers hear this term, they equate it with Jesus claiming humanity. But, the use of this term must be understood in the context of a vision that the Old Testament prophet Daniel saw:

> *I was watching in the night visions,*
> *And behold, One like the Son of Man,*
> *Coming with the clouds of heaven!*
> *He came to the Ancient of Days,*
> *And they brought Him near before Him.*
> *Then to Him was given dominion and glory and a kingdom,*
> *That all peoples, nations, and languages should serve Him.*
> *His dominion is an everlasting dominion,*
> *Which shall not pass away,*
> *And His kingdom the one*
> *Which shall not be destroyed.* (Daniel 7:13-14)

In Daniel's vision, the "Son of Man" is much more than a man. He is the One before whom the whole world bows to worship. When Jesus said of His coming again, *"Then they will see the Son of Man coming in a cloud with power and great glory"* (Luke 21:27), He was clearly referencing this vision. When Jesus called Himself "Son of Man," His listeners knew He was equating Himself with Almighty God.

3. Jesus called Himself the "Son of God." When Jesus heard His friend Lazarus was sick, He said, *"This sickness is not unto death, but for the glory of God, that the Son of God may be glorified through it"* (John 11:4). When the religious Jews heard Jesus use the term "Son of God" in speaking of Himself, they immediately knew He was claiming much more than to be *a* son of God. The Jews would not kill someone for claiming to be a son of God. But Jesus claimed to be *the* Son of God, and therefore divine. It was for this reason they wanted to kill Him. They said, *"We have a law, and according to our law He ought to die, because He made Himself the Son of God"* (John 19:7).

4. Jesus claimed to be one with God the Father. Jesus told His disciples, *"If you had known Me, you would have known My Father also; and from now on you know Him and have seen Him"* (John 14:7). In the next verse, Jesus says, *"If you have seen me, you have seen the Father."* At another time, when He was speaking in the temple in Jerusalem, Jesus said, *"I and My Father are one"* (John 10:30). When the religious Jews heard Him say this, it is obvious that they understood Him to be claiming to be God because they immediately tried to kill Him: *"The Jews answered Him, saying, 'For a good work we do not stone You, but for blasphemy, and because You, being a Man, make Yourself God'"* (John 10:33).

5. Jesus claimed to have ultimate authority. Jesus said, *"All authority has been given to Me in heaven and on earth"* (Matthew 28:18). How could Jesus claim all authority unless He was also claiming to be God?

6. Jesus allowed others to worship Him. The first of the Ten Commandments states: *"You shall have no other gods before Me"* (Exodus 20:3). Accordingly, the worst heresy for a Jew to teach was the worship of anyone other than the One True God. Yet, Jesus accepted the worship of His disciples. When Peter, responding to Jesus' question of

"Who do you say that I am?" said, *"You are the Christ the Son of the Living God,"* Jesus did not stop him as any good Jew was instantly bound to do. Instead He said to Peter, *"Blessed are you, Simon Bar Jonah, for flesh and blood has not revealed this to you, but My Father who is in heaven"* (Matthew 16:15-17).

Thomas doubted that Jesus rose from the dead and he demanded proof. He said, *"Unless I see in His hands the print of the nails, and put my finger into the print of the nails, and put my hand into His side, I will not believe"* (John 20:25). Eight days later, Jesus suddenly appeared where the disciples were gathered. Jesus offered His hands for Thomas to examine. Thomas responded by crying out, *"My Lord and my God!"* (John 20:28). Thomas worshipped Jesus and Jesus did not rebuke him or tell him he was worshipping the wrong person; instead, Jesus accepted the worship as His rightful due.

7. Jesus claimed to be the Alpha and the Omega. In the book of Revelation, Jesus is revealed to the Apostle John in all His glory:

> *In the midst of the seven lampstands One like the Son of Man, clothed with a garment down to the feet and girded about the chest with a golden band. His head and hair were white like wool, as white as snow, and His eyes like a flame of fire; His feet were like fine brass, as if refined in a furnace, and His voice as the sound of many waters; He had in His right hand seven stars, out of His mouth went a sharp two-edged sword, and His countenance was like the sun shining in its strength.* (Revelation 1:13-16)

John writes, *"Then I saw a great white throne and Him who sat on it, from whose face the earth and the heaven fled away..."* (Revelation 20:11). The figure on the throne says to John, *"It is done! I am the Alpha and the Omega, the Beginning and the End"* (Revelation 21:6). When Jesus claims to be the Alpha and the Omega, He is claiming to be the A to the Z and everything in between, the beginning to the end, the One who created the world, and the One who judges the world at the end. In John's vision, Jesus is awe inspiring and deserving of all glory, honor, and praise.

Jesus acted like God

Not only did Jesus claim to be God with His words, He also acted in ways that only God could act.

1. Jesus forgave sins, an act only God can do. Jesus said, *"The Son of Man has authority on earth to forgive sins"* (Matthew 9:6). By claiming the ability to forgive sins, Jesus was claiming to be God. Once when a paralyzed man was brought to Him, Jesus said to the man, *"Son, your sins are forgiven you."* The religious Jews who heard Him said to themselves, *"Why does this man speak blasphemies like this? Who can forgive sins, but God alone?"* Jesus who understood their thoughts, replied to them, *"Which is easier, to say to the paralytic, 'Your sins are forgiven you,' or to say, 'Arise, take up your bed and walk'?"* Then He healed the sick man as proof of His power to forgive sins (Mark 2:5-11).

2. Jesus controlled nature. He caused a storm to be stilled by saying, *"Peace be still"* (Mark 4:39). When was the last time a mere man could control the wind and the waves with his words?

3. Jesus raised the dead. He raised Lazarus from the dead by saying, *"Come forth"* (John 11:43). If you try that at the next funeral you attend, people will think you are crazy. But they wouldn't think so anymore if the dead person sat up.

4. Jesus promised to do what only God can do. He claimed that He would return to judge the world (Matthew 25:31-32).

The Biblical evidence is clear, not only did Jesus claim to be God, He also acted like God. But, even if someone claims to be God, while it's possible that the claim could be true, it's also very possible he could be lying or he might even be crazy. Which one was Jesus? Let's take a look at these three options.

A liar, a lunatic or the Lord God?

Jesus is either bad, mad, or God. C.S. Lewis, in *Mere Christianity*, proposes the liar, lunatic, or Lord trilemma. Lewis wrote:

> *You must make your choice. Either this man was, and is, the Son of God: or else a madman or something worse. You can shut Him up for a fool, you can spit at Him and kill Him as a demon or you can fall at His feet and call Him Lord and God. But let us not come with any patronizing nonsense about His being a great human teacher. He has not left that open to us. He did not intend to.[1]*

Was Jesus a Liar? Jesus claimed to be God and even acted like He was God. Is it possible that Jesus made up the story about being God to gain attention, power, or money? If it was for any of these reasons, He must have been disappointed in the result. From all we know, while He was not a poor beggar, He was not wealthy. While He was popular for a short time, He was crucified with hardly anyone to mourn His death. The attention that His claims got Him eventually led to His execution. If He had simply renounced His claims of divinity, He would never have been crucified. Most people who are lying stop the dishonesty when their life hangs in the balance.

For centuries, even non-Christians have recognized the beauty and power of Jesus' teaching. Gandhi, the father of modern India, said, "To me, [Jesus] was one of the greatest teachers humanity has ever had."[2] It would be a strange ethical teacher who built his reputation on a foundation of lies. Jesus cannot be both a chronic liar and a great moral teacher.

Was Jesus a Lunatic? Admittedly, some of the things Jesus said sound a little crazy. There are crazy people in the world and sometimes they say similarly crazy things. Perhaps you've heard the joke about the two inmates in the psychiatric hospital: Once there was a man in a lunatic asylum who claimed to be Moses reincarnated. The psychologist came into his cell and asked him, "Why do you think you are Moses?" The man explained, "I know I'm Moses incarnated because that's what God said." From the next cell came the voice of another inmate who said, "I never said that."

A sane person knows he or she is not creator of the universe, but Jesus claimed to be exactly that. Evidence against Him being crazy rests in the miracles that Jesus performed. A lunatic may claim to be able to heal the sick, but Jesus actually healed the sick. A lunatic might claim to be able to rise from the dead, but only true divinity can come back from the grave.

As His moral teachings prove that Jesus is no liar, they also prove that He was not insane. Thomas Jefferson, the author of the Declaration of Independence and the third president of the United States, was a Deist who accepted Christ's moral teaching but rejected His miracles. Jefferson used scissors to cut all the supernatural accounts out of the Gospels, but he kept all the teachings of Jesus. Yes, Jesus was a great teacher, but if His teachings are taken seriously, His claims to divinity must be taken just as seriously. Jesus cannot be both a great moral teacher and a lunatic.

Jesus is Lord

The trilemma is solved. Jesus is not a liar. Jesus is not crazy. The only option left of the three is that He is Lord. He is who He claimed to be: the Creator of the Universe, the Son of God. The ultimate proof that Jesus is who He claimed to be is the fact that He rose from the dead.

The fact that Jesus claimed to be God and actually provided proof that He is God by rising from the dead, once again shows me that: God CARES!

CHAPTER 13
The Resurrection of Jesus

Premise A: *People do not rise from the dead.*

Premise B: *God could rise from the dead.*

Premise C: *Jesus rose from the dead.*

Conclusion: *Therefore, Jesus is God.*

I love a popular hymn that Christians sing:

> *I serve a risen Savior, He's in the world today;*
> *I know that He is living, whatever men may say.*
> *I see His hand of mercy, I feel His voice of cheer;*
> *And just the time I need Him, He's always near.*
> *He lives, He lives, Christ Jesus lives today…*

This song celebrates the central fact of the Christian faith: the resurrection of Jesus from the dead. According to Paul, Christianity rises and falls on the resurrection of Christ. He writes, *"If Christ has not been raised, our preaching is useless and so is your faith"* (1 Corinthians 15:14). If Jesus was simply a first century teacher whose bones rotted away in the grave, then there is no harm in ignoring His teaching. If Jesus did not come back from the dead, there is no point in talking about the atonement, or eschatology, or ecclesiology, or any of the other subjects that theologians love to debate. But if Jesus did rise from the dead, the implications are enormous. A resurrected Jesus is proof that He is who He claimed to be. A resurrected Jesus is proof the Bible is true. A resurrected Jesus is proof that His teachings must be taken seriously.

Throughout history, there have been many founders of different religions—like Buddha, Moses, Mohammad, Confucius and Joseph Smith. Jesus is unique in history as a religious leader because of the claim that He would rise from the dead. All the other religious leaders have died and stayed dead. Buddha, Moses, Mohammad, Confucius and Joseph Smith are all dead. But Christianity claims that Jesus is alive. How can we know if Jesus really rose from the dead? Let's look at the evidence.

Evidence that Jesus rose from the dead

The resurrection of Jesus is not a repeatable experiment. One cannot kill Jesus again and scientifically observe the resurrection in the laboratory. The resurrection of Jesus was a one-time event that must be judged through the lens of historical reports. It is in this arena that there is a great deal of evidence for the resurrection.

1. Jesus was crucified. All four Gospels agree on this fact as well as the writings of Paul and the book of Acts. Non-Christian sources also agree. The crucifixion is recorded by Josephus, Tacitus, Lucian, Mara Bar-Serapion, and by the Talmud. But was it a cruci-fiction or crucifixion? One of the Jesus Seminar scholars who is highly skeptical of the life of Jesus, John Dominic Crossan, writes, "That he was crucified is as sure as anything historical can be." E.M. Blaiklock, professor of Classics at Auckland University said, "I tell you that the evidence for the life, the death, and the resurrection of Christ is better authenticated than most of the facts of ancient history."

2. Jesus' disciples absolutely believed that He rose from the dead. During the trial that preceded the crucifixion, the disciples of Jesus were so afraid that they ran away and hid themselves from the Jewish leaders. It was fear that caused Peter to deny Jesus three times. But after the resurrection, the disciples became fearless and preached about Jesus in the Temple courts, to the dismay of the Jewish leaders.

What caused such a dramatic change? The disciples had seen a risen Jesus with their own eyes.

So convinced were the disciples that Jesus was alive, they were willing to give their own lives because of their belief. The disciples suffered humiliation, torture, imprisonment, and martyrdom for their belief that Jesus rose from the dead. Of the eleven disciples who witnessed the resurrection, all but one (John), were martyred for their faith. When threatened with death, none of them recanted or denied their beliefs. It is hard to believe they would have given their lives for the sake of a lie.

Eyewitness testimony proves Jesus rose from the dead. The resurrected Jesus was seen by a variety of individuals and groups. Jesus showed Himself alive with many "infallible proofs" over a period of forty days (Acts 1:3). He appeared to two disciples on the road to Emmaus (Luke 24:13-32), to the eleven disciples hiding behind closed doors (John 20:19-23, 26-29; Mark 16:4-8; Luke 24:36-52), to some of His disciples who had returned to their fishing nets after the crucifixion (John 21:1-14), to Peter (1 Corinthians 15:5), to five hundred of His followers at one time (1 Corinthians 15:6), to James (1 Corinthians 15:7), to a group of disciples at the time of His ascension into heaven (Luke 24:50), and to Paul at his conversion (Acts 9:5; 1 Corinthians 15:8). The many eye-witness testimonies give strong credibility to the fact of the resurrection. No court would dismiss the evidence of hundreds of people.

3. Great skeptics became great believers. James and Jude, the brothers of Jesus, and Saul, who was to become the Apostle Paul, are three examples of people who did not believe in Jesus before the proof of His resurrection. All were radically changed by the clear belief that Jesus rose from the dead. For James and Jesus' other brothers, it must have been a challenge to have such a special brother. What is obvious from Scripture is that James and his brothers did not initially believe Jesus' claims to be the Son of God. That changed after the resurrection. James became an important figure of the church in Jerusalem. He was later killed for his belief. He and his brother Jude each contributed a book to the New Testament.

Saul had no reason to become a Christian. He came from a well-regarded family in a wealthy city. He was trained by one of the greatest rabbis in Jewish history, Gamaliel. He was so zealous for the law of Moses and his Jewish traditions that he went around killing Christians. At the rate he was going, he was destined to become one of the religious leaders of Judaism. Yet, he threw away all of it—his reputation, his wealth, his status, and his position—to join his enemies, the Christians, because of his encounter with the resurrected Jesus. Because of his new faith in Jesus, he was willing to travel thousands of miles in horrible conditions to preach the Gospel, be stoned, beaten, shipwrecked, imprisoned, and ultimately to be executed. He willingly suffered hardship, torture, and persecution so that he could proclaim that Jesus had risen from the dead.

4. The tomb was empty. Jesus was publicly crucified and placed inside the tomb of Joseph of Arimathea, a member of the Sanhedrin. Roman soldiers were posted at the tomb with strict instructions to prevent anyone from taking the body. Three days later, the tomb was empty. The disciples were accused of stealing the body, but it is a fact that the body was not in the tomb. The Jewish leaders could have instantly quashed the sect of Christianity by producing Christ's body. The fact they did not is proof that His body was gone.

5. The first witnesses were women. Women were considered unreliable witnesses in first century Jewish society, so if someone was making up a story about Christ's resurrection, they would not have made up a story about women finding Him first. But this is in fact what the Gospels record—that women were the first ones to see the empty tomb and to see the resurrected Savior. The men did not at first believe them and went to the tomb themselves. What they saw—an empty tomb—only confirmed the testimony of the women.

6. Only Christ's resurrection from the dead can account for the rapid growth of the early church. While Christianity is prominent today, Jesus was an obscure religious teacher in a forgotten corner of the Roman Empire. Yet He started a movement that changed the empire and the world. The reason for the impact of Christianity is that Jesus rose from the dead.

Five explanations for the resurrection

Atheists and non-believers object to the resurrection by asserting that people do not rise from the dead. Because people do not come back from the dead, then Jesus did not rise from the dead. This objection is based on a worldview that rejects the supernatural. But if one's worldview rejects the possibility of miracles, the existence of God, and the facts of Christianity, then one must come up with an alternate explanation to account for the historical evidence of the resurrection. There is a set of "minimal facts" about the resurrection of Jesus that almost all scholars, both believers and unbelievers, agree on and that must be explained.[1] These facts are as follows:

1. Jesus died by crucifixion and was buried.

2. Jesus' tomb was empty, and His body was missing.

3. The disciples had actual experiences of what they thought were real appearances of a risen Jesus and they genuinely believed He had risen from the dead.

4. The lives of the disciples were completely changed by their experience of a risen Jesus to the point that they were willing to give their lives for their new-found faith.

5. The tradition of Christ's resurrection was communicated very early.

6. Men like James, the unbelieving brother of Jesus, and Paul, the persecutor of believers, became believers because of meeting what they thought was the resurrected Jesus.

Let's consider five explanations of the resurrection of Jesus and how they stand up to these minimal facts.

1. The Swoon Theory. This theory proposes that Jesus did not really die on the cross; He only passed out and was later revived. This theory is problematic for a few reasons. First, the Romans knew how to kill people. People crucified by the Romans did not survive. Second, even if Jesus could have lived through the crucifixion, there is no way He could have escaped the tomb in His weakened condition. When the Jews buried their dead, they wound them up in strips of cloth, binding their hands and feet. The difficulty of getting free of His graveclothes would have been extraordinary for any man, and much more so for Jesus who had been crucified. Of course, if He had managed to do so, in the mouth of the tomb where He was buried was an enormous stone, and beyond it was a guard of Roman soldiers. It would have been impossible for Jesus to move the stone or sneak past the guards. Third, even if Jesus had survived the crucifixion and managed to escape the tomb, His body would have been in such a horrible state that no one would have mistaken Him for being resurrected. The people who saw Jesus reported that He had a glorified, resurrected body, not a body recovering from a crippling ordeal.

2. The Conspiracy Theory. In this scenario, the resurrection is a deception perpetrated by some disciples who stole Jesus' body. Some objections to this theory are that, first, if it was a conspiracy, how did the disciples steal the body? It was being guarded by Roman soldiers. The guards knew their lives would be forfeited if they failed in their assignment to guard the body. Second, as mentioned above, the disciples all gave their lives for their belief in the risen Christ. People may lie for personal profit, but few people continue the lie when their lives are on the line.

3. The Hallucination Theory. This hypothesis suggests that the disciples hallucinated about a resurrected Jesus. Jesus was still dead and still in the tomb; their belief in His resurrection was simply the product of their overactive imaginations. Problems to this hypothesis include, first, that there was little precedent for thinking that someone could come back from the dead. The Pharisees believed there would be a general resurrection at the end of time, but no one imagined that an individual would resurrect. Second, some of the people who witnessed the resurrected Christ were not His disciples before the resurrection. They only became disciples because of witnessing His resurrection. Third, the reports of Christ's resurrection are not of the type that can be produced by a hallucination. Hallucinations are always individual occurrences, but Jesus was often seen by groups of people, and in one instance, over five hundred people saw Jesus at one time.

4. The Legend Theory. By this theory, the account of Jesus' resurrection is a legend, a myth that grew up over a long period of time. The primary objection to this theory is simply that the written record does not bear it out. The time between the death of Jesus and the written records of His resurrection is short. Paul wrote 1 Corinthians within twenty years of Jesus' resurrection. The witnesses to the resurrection that he mentions were still alive and available for anyone to interview. Paul's words are written too soon to be myth. He regards the resurrection as a verifiable historical fact.

5. The Truth. Jesus really rose from the dead. The evidence rules out all natural options that explain away the resurrection, leaving only the supernatural to account for the resurrection that so convinced the first Christians. As Arthur Conan Doyle's Sherlock Holmes famously said, "Once you eliminate the impossible, whatever remains, no matter how improbable, must be the truth." As N.T. Wright says, "The proposal that Jesus was bodily raised from the dead possesses unrivaled power to explain the historical data at the heart of early Christianity."[2]

Some people dismiss the story of Jesus as nothing but a fairy tale or a myth, but I like what C.S. Lewis said after J.R.R. Tolkien witnessed to him. He wrote, "The story of Christ is simply a true myth: a myth working on us in the same way as the others, but with this tremendous difference that it really happened." The implications of the historical evidence are enormous. They are that Jesus rose from the dead, that Jesus is the God He says He is, and that what the Bible says about God, creation, sin, judgment, eternity, and heaven and hell are true. Two more implications of the resurrection are:

That, yes, indeed, God CARES for you. And that because He cares for you, you have a choice to make.

PROOF

PART 3:
DO I DARE?

Deciding to Trust in God

CHAPTER 14
Choosing Truth

You shall know the truth, and the truth shall make you free. — John 8:32

Pontius Pilate, the Roman Governor presiding over the trial of Jesus, asked the question, *"What is truth?"* (John 18:38). Philosophers throughout time have asked and debated the same question. Have you ever asked yourself this question?

What is truth?

Philosophically, there are two different approaches to the idea of truth. The first approach proposes that truth-with-a-capital-T exists, the other approach denies there is such a thing as ultimate truth. The first type of truth is objective truth. An objective truth is a fact that is true for everyone everywhere at all times. Plato, the Greek philosopher, suggested the idea of universal truth. For something to be true, it must correspond to reality. For it to be universally true, it must take in the whole universe and be true in all dimensions of time and space.

An example of objective or universal truth would be mathematics. The logic of mathematics requires that 2+2=4. There is no time in history that 2+2 did not equal 4. If I have two apples and then I add two more apples, I will have four apples. When I add two apples to two apples, it is impossible for me to have three apples or five apples. This logic works no matter what is being added—apples or oranges—and it doesn't matter where in the universe or when in history the addition is being done. Nor does mathematics change because of people's beliefs. A child who is learning addition might believe that 2+2=5. But no amount of believing makes that answer true. Even if people didn't exist to do math, the answer to the question would always be 4.

An objective truth does not change with different perspectives. For example, witnesses to a car wreck may have many different perspectives of the accident, but there is only one truth about what happened. One witness may say the car ran a red light and another witness may say the light was green. While both witnesses have a perspective, there is only one objective truth: either the light was red, or it was green. Because of objective truth, there can be no such thing as a red-green light, a round square, a male woman, or a good murder. Objectivity refers to point-of-view and what is true despite the different points of view that may be represented. Objective truth is stable and unchanging. Where truth is stable and unchanging, the opposite of truth is error.

The second type of truth is subjective truth. Subjective truth refers to the idea that a fact is true for only one person or one group of people. According to J. Warner Wallace objective truth is rooted in the nature of the object under consideration and transcends the opinions of any subject considering this object, and subjective truth is rooted in the opinions and beliefs of the subjects who hold them and vary from person to person. For example, I think it is true that vanilla ice cream is superior to chocolate ice cream. However, my wife, who likes chocolate ice cream better, disagrees with me. My opinion about ice cream is a subjective truth because it depends upon what a subject (me) thinks and not on what the object is (the ice cream). The fact that ice cream is a cold dessert made from milk and sugar is an objective truth, but the idea that one flavor of ice cream tastes better than another is a subjective truth.

Subjectivity, like objectivity, refers to point of view. A subjective truth is based on a person's feelings, perspective, or opinion. Because subjective truth is based on opinion, something may be true in one culture but not in another culture. For example, in Western culture, it is a shared belief that it is rude to be more than five minutes late to a meeting. But, in many other cultures it is acceptable to arrive an hour late to a meeting, or even later. So the claim that it is rude to be five minutes late to a meeting is only subjectively true since it does not apply in all contexts or to all people.

This subjective approach to truth leads to a philosophy of relativism. Relativism is "the belief that knowledge, truth, and morality exist in relation to culture, society, or historical context, and are not absolute." To the relativist, as society and culture changes, truth also changes. For example, in American culture, living together before marriage used to be frowned upon as an improper thing, but now so many people live together before they get married that most people no longer think it is wrong. Because of examples like this, relativists claim that truth is not stable, and that absolute truth does not exist. So when it comes to Christianity those who adopt a relativist approach to truth might say something like, "Christianity may be true for you, but it is not true for me."

The problem with relativism

However, when relativists say that no belief is true for everyone, they are making a statement that they believe is true for everyone. Their position ironically refutes itself since they are making a universal claim that no universal claim is true. Post-modern relativism has a hard time establishing its truth claims because it frequently contradicts itself. For example, the claim "everything is meaningless" is assumed to be a meaningful statement. Relativism abounds with these kinds of statements:

- "There is no truth." This statement is obviously claiming to be a true statement.
- "There are no absolutes." This statement makes an absolute claim.
- "All truth is relative." If this is the case, this statement is also relative.

- "You can't know anything for sure." Including if this statement is true.
- "Everything is meaningless." If that is true, this statement is meaningless.

Statements like these demonstrate relativism's weakness as a belief system. Relativists are like the people Paul mentions in Romans 1:22: *"Professing to be wise, they became fools."* Truth exists, even if no one knows it, believes it, or accepts it. Truth does not depend upon majority opinion. At one time, most people in the world believed the sun revolved around the earth, but just because people believed this, it did not make it true. William Penn wrote, "Right is right, even if everyone is against it. And wrong is wrong, even if everyone is for it." Truth is not created, it is discovered.

Is science truth?

Medieval theologian, Thomas Aquinas, called theology "the queen of the sciences."[1] In his day, all scientific study was subordinated to the theologian's higher research into the nature of God. The temporal natural world was of a lower order than the eternal and supernatural. Theology was queen because it sought to discover ultimate truth.

But today, theology has been dethroned, and many scientists believe that science and theology should not mix. For the "new atheists," the reason they should not mix is that the two are directly opposed. Sam Harris writes, "The conflict between religion and science is unavoidable. The success of science often comes at the expense of religious dogma; the maintenance of religious dogma always comes at the expense of science."[2] Christopher Hitchens wrote, "All attempts to reconcile faith with science and reason are consigned to failure and ridicule."[3] Richard Dawkins said, "I am hostile to fundamentalist religion because it actively debauches the scientific enterprise [...] It subverts science and saps the intellect."[4] Atheists generally look to science as the source of ultimate truth.

The conflict between science and religion is due to a misunderstanding of the realms they explore and roles they play. Some atheists believe religion is mainly an attempt to explain the unexplainable in nature. From this they argue that the more science explains, the less there is for religion to explain. For example, some atheists believe religion was originally invented by cavemen to explain thunder and lightning. Now that science has discovered the natural explanations for these natural phenomena, religion has one less thing to explain. But such a perspective only acknowledges a natural world that can be scientifically observed. If human knowledge was limited to what was observable scientifically, then the atheists could be correct. But theology and its cousin philosophy remain important because human experience and knowledge is larger than science. Science can answer questions about *how*, but only philosophy and theology can answer the questions of *why*.

Science is good at answering the "how" questions. The scientific method forms a hypothesis and then tests the hypothesis through experimentation. The results of the experiment are analyzed. If the evidence shows the hypothesis is false, then a new hypothesis must be formed and tested. The near-religious belief in science and its methods that many atheists and others hold is called scientism or logical positivism. This perspective claims that if something cannot be proved in the laboratory, it should not be believed. The problem with such thinking is that it fails to acknowledge the limitations of science for covering areas of knowledge that cannot be scientifically examined— such as history, ethics, aesthetics, philosophy, and religious experience.

For example, it is impossible to do experiments in the laboratory to prove historical events. Using science, one cannot prove that George Washington was the first president of the United States or that Ronald Reagan was the 40th. One cannot prove that Julius Caesar or Shakespeare ever lived. One cannot prove scientifically that Jesus rose from the dead. The facts of His existence or His resurrection are not a repeatable experiment.

There are many things that humans know that can never be scientifically tested. Science can measure the saliva transfer that happens during a kiss, but not the love of two individuals. Science can predict the exact time of the sunset, but it cannot explain why it is beautiful. Science can unwrap the DNA helix, but it cannot tell us why we are here on this earth. Science can discover ever more effective ways for us to kill people, but science has no ability to tell us why we should not kill. Science is good at answering the question of *how*, but it often doesn't have an answer for *why*.

Answering the question of *why* is the role of religion. Galileo (1564-1642), the scientist, astronomer, and theologian, wrote: "The Bible shows the way to go to heaven, not the way the heavens go." Isaac Newton said, "Gravity explains the motions of the planets, but it cannot explain who set the planets in motion." Science can explain natural things, but it cannot explain the supernatural. It can explain the observable, but not what is unseen. It can explain the human body, but it cannot perform experiments on the human spirit. For this reason, science has not disproven miracles. In fact, it is impossible for science to disprove miracles. Science deals exclusively with the natural world and does not acknowledge a supernatural world. A miracle, by definition, is something that does not happen naturally.

Because human experience is larger than science, science cannot be the source of ultimate truth. Believing that science has the answers to all of life's questions may seem comforting, but as Carl Sagan, an atheist and scientist said, "It is far better to grasp the universe as it really is than to persist in delusion however satisfying or reassuring."[5] To insist that science is the source of ultimate truth is to persist in a delusion.

Ultimately, there should be no conflict between theology and science. Both are concerned with seeking truth. Albert Einstein said, "A legitimate conflict between science and religion cannot exist. Science without religion is lame, religion without science is blind." Certainly, science has been a great blessing to society. Because of scientific progress the world enjoys electricity, motorized transport, and cell phones. Science has cured tuberculosis, given us vaccines, and extended our life spans. But for all the good things that science has achieved, it has also enabled great evil. From gunpowder, to land mines, to atomic bombs, to unmanned drones, science has continually invented more efficient ways of killing other humans. Crimes, like identity theft and many forms of fraud are enabled by the technologies created from science. Science doesn't have the power to set the world free from evil. Truth, not science, is the remedy for error.

How can I know truth?

According to Ravi Zacharias, there are three tests for truth:[6] logical consistency, empirical adequacy, and experiential relevance.

1. Logical consistency. Are there any contradictions? Logical consistency means the truth must be logical, it must make sense. An object cannot be both A and not-A at the same time. Truth must be internally consistent. A fact is either true or it is not true. Aristotle wrote, "To say of what is that it is not, or of what is not that it is, is false, while to say of what is that it is, and of what is not that it is not, is true; so that he who says of anything that it is, or that it is not, will say either what is true or what is false." For example, a door can either be open or closed. It cannot be both open and closed at the same time. If a door is open, then it is not closed and if it is closed, it is not open. If one person believes a door is open and another person believes the door is closed, one of them is wrong. Two or more contradictory statements cannot both be true.

2. Empirical adequacy. Is there any proof? A worldview should be supported by evidence when it is tested. The truth must pertain in a meaningful way to reality. One's beliefs should reflect the way the universe actually is. We can know a truth is true if it matches reality. A truth cannot become truth just because someone believes it is true. I may believe I have gasoline in my car, but this belief cannot make my car run if the gasoline tank is empty. Even if I start a political movement and convince lots of people that my car is full of gas, people's belief that the car is full of gas does not make it so.

3. Experiential relevance. Does it work in real life? In a pragmatic way, truth should work in our everyday lives. This is a major reason why I am a Christian: of all the religions, Christianity does the best job of describing the way the world actually works and it describes humans as they really are.

Does the existence of objective truth prove the existence of God?

Saint Augustine argued for the existence of God from unchanging, objective, universal truth.[7] Here is how his argument went:

Premise A:	*There are timeless and unchanging truths.*
Premise B:	*There must be a cause for these truths.*
Premise C:	*This cause must be equal to, lesser than, or greater than our minds.*
Premise D:	*This cause cannot be equal to our minds, since these truths are independent of our minds (our minds are subject to them).*
Premise E:	*These truths cannot be lesser than our minds, since our minds are subject to them.*
Premise F:	*These truths must be greater than our changeable minds.*
Premise G	*Whatever is superior to the changeable is itself unchangeable.*
Conclusion:	*Therefore, there is an unchanging Mind, which is the source of unchanging truth.*

The existence or non-existence of God is an objective truth. Either God is there, or God is not there. The resurrection of Christ is another objective truth. Paul puts a great deal of emphasis on the truth of Christ's resurrection in 1 Corinthians 15:14-19. Christ's resurrection is not a matter subject to interpretation; it either happened or it did not happen. Either Jesus is the Savior of all humankind, or He is just a religious teacher who lived two thousand years ago. In this book, I have presented various proofs for the existence of God and for the resurrection of Christ. Now, it is your job to decide if the things I have discussed are true or not true.

Jesus is truth personified

Truth is important to God. Because truth is important to Him, He does not lie (Hebrews 6:18), His Word is called truth (John 17:17), the Holy Spirit is called the *"spirit of truth"* (John 14:17) and Jesus is *"full of grace and truth"* (John 1:14). The philosophers of today may deny that there is truth, or if there is truth, they may deny that it can be known. But Jesus said, *"I am the way, the truth, and the life"* (John 14:6). Ultimately, to know Jesus is to know the truth.

Will you DARE to believe in Him?

PROOF

CHAPTER 15
Choosing Faith

Jesus answered and said to them, "Have faith in God." — Mark 11:22

Atheists often ridicule Christians for their faith. Atheists ask, "Is faith a reliable guide to truth?" They answer by saying, "No!" This is because atheists define "religious faith" as "believing without evidence" or "pretending to know things you don't know."[1] Richard Dawkins wrote: "Faith is the great cop-out, the great excuse to evade the need to think and evaluate evidence. Faith is belief in spite of, even perhaps because of, the lack of evidence."[2] Or, as Mark Twain said, "Faith is believing what you know ain't so."[3]

Atheists ask, "If there are ten million gods, and the worshippers of all of the gods all claim faith as their reason for believing, how can you claim that your faith is unique?" They say the main problem with faith is that it can be used to believe literally anything. What good is faith if it can lead to any conclusion? However, the atheist's definition of faith and the biblical definition of faith are different. When the atheist speaks of faith, he is talking about "wishful thinking," a faith that chooses to believe in something in spite of evidence to the contrary. But the faith spoken of in the Bible is belief based on solid evidence.

Biblical faith is based on evidence

Throughout the Old Testament, God revealed Himself to the people of Israel through physical manifestations. To set them free, He sent plagues on the Egyptians and He parted the Red Sea. He provided for them in the desert by sending them manna every day for forty years and by causing fresh water to flow from rocks. He appeared to them in a cloud and as a pillar of fire. When they arrived in the Promised Land, He gave them victory by bringing down the rock walls of Jericho. The Israelites had tangible evidence of God's existence.

In the New Testament, Jesus offers many tangible proofs of His deity.

- When John the Baptist was thrown into prison, he wondered if Jesus really was the Messiah he had thought Him to be. Jesus did not tell John's disciples go back to John the Baptist and say to him, "Just have faith." Instead, Jesus told them to talk about the miracles they were witnessing: *"Jesus answered and said to them, "Go and tell John the things which you hear and see: The blind see and the lame walk; the lepers are cleansed and the deaf hear; the dead are raised up and the poor have the gospel preached to them"* (Matthew 11:4-5).
- When the Pharisees questioned if Jesus has the authority to forgive sins, Jesus proved His deity by healing the paralyzed man (Matthew 9:2-8).
- When Jesus rose from the dead, He revealed Himself to the disciples, He ate food with them, and He invited doubting Thomas to touch the holes in His hands. *"When He had said this, He showed them His hands and His feet. But while they still did not believe for joy, and marveled, He said to them, "Have you any food here?" So they gave Him a piece of a broiled fish and some honeycomb. And He took it and ate in their presence"* (Luke 24:40-43).
- After His resurrection, Jesus appeared to over five hundred people, giving those, who had seen Him die, proof that He was indeed alive again: *"To whom He also presented Himself alive after His suffering by many infallible proofs, being seen by*

them during forty days and speaking of the things pertaining to the kingdom of God" (Acts 1:3).

The Bible does not teach "blind faith." The Greek word *tekmērion* translated in Acts 1:3 as "many convincing proofs" is a word used in court to refer to "proof beyond a reasonable doubt." In other words, in the forty days between the resurrection and the ascension, Jesus proved that He had risen from the dead. Jim Burkett asks, "Was it the resurrection that caused the disciples to have faith or was it faith that caused the disciples to believe in the resurrection?" The answer is that the faith of the disciples was based on their experience that Jesus actually rose from the dead. As the Apostle John wrote: *"That...which we have heard, which we have seen with our eyes, which we have looked upon, and our hands have handled...that which we have seen and heard we declare to you"* (1 John 1:1-3). The early church saw Jesus alive, and this fact became the foundation for their faith. Christianity is a factual faith.

It is true that, *"without faith it is impossible to please God"* (Hebrews 11:6), but this faith is based on the *"evidence of things we do not see"* (Hebrews 11:1). Have you ever read a detective story or watched a criminal investigation series on TV? By carefully examining a crime scene, the sleuth or investigator reconstructs what happened during the crime. Tiny clues provide evidence of events not seen. Faith is the same: from the things which can be seen it provides absolute proof of things we cannot see. The Apostle Paul explains:

> *For the invisible things of Him from the creation of the world are clearly seen, being understood by the things that are made, even His eternal power and Godhead; so that they are without excuse: because that, when they knew God, they glorified Him not as God, neither were thankful; but became vain in their imaginations, and their foolish heart was darkened. Professing themselves to be wise, they became fools...* (Romans 1:20-22)

In this passage, Paul says that those who do not believe in God are without excuse because of the overwhelming evidence of creation. Paul calls atheists "fools" because they choose to ignore the evidence of the things which can be seen. For those who are willing to look, there is more than enough evidence for God's existence. God has left a bread trail of crumbs that lead directly to the Bread of Life.

Faith based on experience

Not only is Biblical faith based on evidence, it is also based on experience. For example, when I sit down in a chair, I have faith the chair is strong enough to hold me. However, this belief is not blind faith or wishful thinking, instead it is based on a lifetime of experience. In my dining room, there is a chair that I have sat in hundreds of times. Today's trust in my chair is based on yesterday's experience when that chair did not collapse when I sat down. In the same way, Christians have faith in God because of His faithfulness.

We all live by faith in our everyday lives. When I get on an airplane, I put my faith in the pilot to fly me to my destination. When I purchase food from the supermarket, I have faith it will nourish me. When I go to work, I have faith my wife is not running off to sleep with another man. My faith in these various areas is based on past experience. Atheists would say that believing that the sun will rise tomorrow or having faith that a seat can hold your weight would more appropriately be called "trust" or "confidence" because it is based on evidence and experience. In this, Christians concur. Our faith in God is trust and confidence in Him that is based on both evidence and experience. Christians do not have a blind faith that rejects evidence, but a wide-eyed faith that sees and acknowledges the evidence for God.

Christianity is a reasonable faith

There is much in the Christian faith that appears unreasonable: a baby is born to a virgin, a man comes back from the dead, a giant flood covers the whole earth, an angel shuts the mouths of lions. All these miraculous events stand contrary to observed phenomena. But, the faith of the Bible is not antithetical to reason.[4] Christian faith is not willing to believe something despite evidence to the contrary, rather, faith in Christ is built on the foundation of who Jesus is, what He has done, and what He continues to do in the lives of those who believe in Him. If one allows for the evidence and experience that there is a God who can do miracles—as the Bible clearly shows—then Christian faith is reasonable.

Reason and faith are often presented as opponents, especially by atheists. But Christians know that reason is not opposed to faith. Saint Augustine wrote, "I believe in order to understand." He also frequently quoted a version of Isaiah 7:9, *"Unless you believe, you cannot understand."* Augustine said, "Understanding is the reward of faith. Therefore, seek not to understand that you may believe, but believe that you may understand."[5]

Anselm also applied reason to questions of faith. He believed faith was the beginning of knowledge, and that, once someone accepts a truth by faith, she can learn more about it through reason. As a result, one's faith becomes greater as one applies reason to what one believes. He said, "Nor do I seek to understand that I may believe, but I believe that I may understand. For this, too, I believe, that, unless I first believe, I shall not understand."[6]

Aquinas argued that God can be known through both faith and reason. Truth about God is known through two ways: natural revelation and supernatural revelation. Reason discovers what can be known about God from the natural world; faith discovers what can be known about God supernaturally (through the Bible, through miracles, through prayer, and the like). Rather than being opponents, for Aquinas faith and reason were allies.

Both faith and reason can lead to God. However, in matters of faith and reason, one must follow either Plato or Aristotle. Either one begins with faith by receiving "a word from on high," or one begins with reason which is "a word from within." When using faith, a person begins with what God has chosen to reveal and then works their way down from "on high" in order to understand themselves and their world here below. This deductive approach was used by Anselm. When using reason to understand God, a person begins with what is seen with the eyes here "below" and works their way up to understand who God is. This inductive approach was used by Aquinas.[7] In the inductive approach, reason leads to faith; in the deductive approach faith leads to reason. In neither are faith and reason opposed.

According to John Locke, to believe something, apart from reason, is an insult to our Maker, the One who created reason.[8] Galileo wrote, "I do not feel obliged to believe that the same God who endowed us with sense, reason, and intellect had intended for us to forgo their use." The Bible commands Christians to, *"Love the Lord your God... with all your mind"* (Luke 10:27). Thus, the Christian should strive to use, understand, and improve his faculty of reasoning. God wants us to be rational. Reason is not contrary to faith, rather it should be complementary to faith.

Faith is bigger than reason

Most humans do not believe because of reason, they believe because of emotion, feelings, intuitions, prejudices, and impressions. They believe because of what is in their hearts. When the Bible talks about the heart, it isn't referring to the physical organ that pumps blood, but to the center and essence of a person. The Apostle Paul reminds us that it is *"with the heart that one believes"* (Romans 10:10). Because of what is in a Christian's heart, she believes in God. Because of what is in an atheist's heart he does not believe in God. This makes it hard to reason either the Christian or the atheist out of his or her deeply held beliefs. As Jonathan Swift, the Irish author and satirist, pointed out, "It is useless to attempt to reason a man out of a thing he was never reasoned into." Blaise Pascal wrote,

> *The heart has its reasons which reason does not know. We feel it in a thousand things. I say that the heart naturally loves the Universal Being, and also itself naturally, according as it gives itself to them; and it hardens itself against one or the other at its will. You have rejected the one, and kept the other. Is it by reason that you love*

yourself? It is the heart which experiences God, and not the reason. This, then, is faith; God felt by the heart, not by reason.[9]

Faith could be called a "sixth sense." The idea of a sixth sense is a sense that operates beyond our five senses of sight, touch, taste, hearing, and smell. Even so, faith does not go against reason, faith goes beyond reason. By using faith, we sense things in the spiritual realm. When we sense a truth by faith, we do not need to experience it with our other senses to know it is real. This truth can be demonstrated by how we use our other senses. When you see a building off in the distance, you do not doubt it's existence until you are close enough to touch or taste or smell it. No, you believe the building is there even when only one sense confirms that it is real. When you smell a delicious BBQ, you don't need to see the meat roasting before you will believe that someone is cooking a steak.

Faith is similar to the title deed to a property you have never seen. Once the title of a property belongs to you, the property also belongs to you. You can say with assurance, "I own this land" even though you have never seen it. Recently I purchased a plane ticket. When I bought the ticket, I did not demand to see the plane I would be riding in. I had faith the plane would be at the airport when the time arrived for me to leave on my trip. The ticket represented the promise of the airline. Faith is like that ticket; it is the substance that guarantees God's promises will come true. Faith is your ticket to heaven.

We should *"live by faith, not by sight"* (2 Corinthians 5:7). Ultimate proof of God's existence comes from faith. One must use the proper instrument for the object of study. To study the stars, one would not use a microscope. To study an amoeba, one would not use a telescope. The proper instrument for the study of God is faith. Faith is the telescope we look through to see God.

Faith and doubt

It is not wrong to have doubts about God's existence. The truth is that everyone deals with doubts from time to time. But even while experiencing doubt, one can still have faith in God. It is wonderful that you doubt. The capacity that you doubt is the equivalent capacity that you have for faith. If there is no doubt, there is no place for faith to work in your life. If you do not have doubt and uncertainty, then there is no purpose for faith. For example, you can't experience great pleasure unless there has been great pain. In the same way, you cannot experience faith until you have struggled with doubt. René Descartes actually used his doubts as an argument for God.[10] Here is how he argued his point:

Premise A:	*I am doubting and the more I doubt, the more sure I am doubting.*
Premise B:	*If I am doubting, I am thinking since doubting is a form of thinking.*
Premise C:	*But my doubt is an imperfect form of thinking since it lacks certitude.*
Premise D:	*But if I know my thoughts are imperfect, then it means I must be aware of the perfect since I cannot judge something is imperfect unless I know the perfect which it is not.*
Premise E:	*My imperfect mind cannot be the cause of the idea of perfection that I have and by which I judge things to be imperfect.*
Premise F:	*Only a perfect mind is an adequate cause for the idea of perfection.*
Conclusion:	*Therefore, a perfect mind must exist as the cause of my perfect idea. This perfect mind is God.*

Faith doesn't run away from doubt, but towards it. Faith takes courage and bravery. Living what you already know does not take any courage—there is no adventure or risk involved. When you go into the unknown, it is scary, it is suspenseful. Faith is having courage to go into the unknown. The tension between faith and doubt is where life is lived. It is where the ultimate is possible. As an unknown author wrote, "Reason can bring us to the precipice, but only faith can make us leap and fly."

The leap of faith

Once there was a man holding onto a rope dangling off the edge of a tall cliff. He cried out, "Help! Please! Can someone help me?" Suddenly, he heard the voice of God say, "Let go, and I will catch you." The man, looking down, saw nothing but jagged rocks hundreds of feet below. He considered God's offer for a few moments and then shouted, "Is anyone else up there?"

The point of the story is that believing in God ultimately requires a leap of faith. The Danish theologian and existentialist philosopher, Søren Kierkegaard wrote about taking a "leap of faith" into the arms of a loving God.[11] This "leap" is not just mental assent to doctrines for which there is no proof, rather, it is the final step in response to a series of evidences for God's existence.

Even though this leap of faith can be scary and nerve-wracking, it is not a leap into a dark abyss but a step into the light. When I married my wife, Jessica, I had never been married before. I knew I was interested in her, even intrigued by her, but I had no concept of what it meant to be married to a girl. Getting married was a real leap into the unknown, but it was one of the best things I ever did. In the same way, when we decide to put our faith in God, it is a leap into a relationship with the One who created you and the universe.

But you must "pull the trigger" to know how wonderful and good the relationship can be. When my son learned to ride his bike, I carefully explained to him how a bike worked and how to stay balanced. He mentally understood how to ride a bike, but at some point, he had to put his foot on the peddle and push off into the unknown. In the same way, at some point the believer must choose to put his or her faith in God. One tiny step is all it takes, but you must take it.

Believing in God comes down to faith. There is enough evidence for God's existence to justify a person in his or her belief in God. Nonetheless, the very nature of faith requires the unknown. Faith is alive. It is not static. It is existential. Faith is what gets a person across the gap between all the evidence and confident certainty. If you feel you do not have enough faith to believe, it might be helpful to heed the words of the father whose son needed a miracle and said to Jesus, "*Lord, I believe; help my unbelief*" (Mark 9:24).

The Christian life isn't just a moment of faith, but a whole lifetime of faith-filled moments. The more I have said, "Yes" to God, the more faith I have to say, "Yes" to Him again. For every leap of faith that life's moments have brought me, I have always found God on the other side of my faith. Because God has proved Himself faithful to me time and again, when I am faced with new challenges to my faith, I say:

Yes, I DARE to Believe!

CHAPTER 16
High Stakes Choices

I have set before you life and death, blessing and cursing; therefore choose life. — Deuteronomy 30:19

Imagine a conversation between a Christian and an atheist. The Christian begins by asking, "Do you believe in God?"

The Atheist replies, "I don't believe there is a god."

The Christian says, "But, what if you are wrong? If you are wrong, you will spend all of eternity burning in hell. But, if there is a God and you choose to follow Him, then you will spend all of eternity in heaven enjoying yourself forever. Are you willing to take a risk on being wrong?"

The atheist shrugs and says, "Yeah, I am willing to take the risk because if I become a Christian, I would have to stop drinking, and smoking, and having sex with my girlfriend. I think today's pleasure outweighs a potential of infinite pleasure in eternity. Besides, if there is a hell, all my friends are going to hell and I want to party with them!"

"Are you a gambling man?" The Christian replies. "Wouldn't you rather bet on Jesus and increase your chances of winning?"

The atheist says, "I don't believe in god and I don't believe in heaven or hell. I'm not going to lose out on having fun here on earth on the off-chance that there is a god."

The Christian replies, "Do you believe in gravity? It is there whether you believe or not. Even if you say you don't believe in gravity, you will still fall if you jump off a building."

"The existence of gravity can be empirically verified," explains the atheist, "I just don't see any evidence that god is real."

"So, you are willing to risk an eternity of pain in hell if you are wrong?" asks the Christian.

"I just don't see the need to purchase fire insurance for a fire that is probably not real," shrugs the atheist.

The Christian has the final word, "I would rather have insurance and not need it than need it and not have it."

The above conversation, which I actually had, lays out a dilemma that is known as Pascal's Wager.

Pascal's Wager

Blaise Pascal (1623-1662) was an intellectual giant and his inquisitive mind delved into many different disciplines. He was a brilliant scientist, mathematician, inventor, and philosopher. He developed mathematical theorems on geometry and probability theory that are still used today by economists and social scientists and he invented a mechanical calculator. He studied the properties of vacuums and is known for his logic and reasoning. Yet, despite his brilliance, Pascal's life was not an easy one. His mother died when he was three years old and he was sick for most of his adult life. He also had a gambling problem.

At the age of thirty-one, Pascal had a supernatural conversion experience. On November 23, 1654, he was reading John's Gospel, chapter 17, and while he was doing so he had an encounter with the living God. He wrote an account of how he got saved on a piece of paper and had the paper sown into the lining of his coat so that he would always remember the event. This is what he wrote:

> *From about half past ten at night to about half an hour after*
> *midnight, FIRE*
> *"God of Abraham, God of Isaac, God of Jacob," not of philosophers*
> *and scholars*
> *Certitude, heartfelt joy, peace.*
> *God of Jesus Christ.*
> *God of Jesus Christ.*
> *The world forgotten, everything except God.*
> *"O righteous Father, the world has not known You, but I have*
> *known You" (John 17:25)*
> *Joy, joy, joy, tears of joy.*[1]

After his salvation experience, Pascal wrote his *Pensées*, a series of meditations about God and philosophy that were gathered up and published after his death. In this work, Pascal proposed what is known as "Pascal's Wager."

Because of his gambling days and his work on probability theory, Pascal was deeply interested in making bets. In the wager, he bets that it makes more sense to be a Christian than it does to be an atheist. This is what he wrote:

> *Let us then examine this point, and say, "God is, or He is not" But*
> *to which side shall we incline?[...] A game is being played at the*
> *extremity of this infinite distance where heads or tails will turn*
> *up. What will you wager? [...]Yes; but you must wager. It is not*
> *optional [...] Let us weigh the gain and the loss in wagering that*
> *God is. Let us estimate these two chances. If you gain, you gain all;*
> *if you lose, you lose nothing. Wager then without hesitation that He*
> *is. "That is very fine. Yes, I must wager; but I may perhaps wager*
> *too much."—Let us see. Since there is an equal risk of gain and*
> *of loss, if you had only to gain two lives, instead of one, you might*
> *still wager. But if there were three lives to gain, you would have to*

play (since you are under the necessity of playing), and you would be imprudent, when you are forced to play, not to chance your life to gain three at a game where there is an equal risk of loss and gain. But there is an eternity of life and happiness. And this being so, if there were an infinity of chances, of which one only would be for you, you would still be right in wagering one to win two, and you would act stupidly, being obliged to play, by refusing to stake one life against three at a game in which out of an infinity of chances there is one for you, if there were an infinity of an infinitely happy life to gain. But there is here an infinity of an infinitely happy life to gain, a chance of gain against a finite number of chances of loss, and what you stake is finite. It is all divided; wherever the infinite is and there is not an infinity of chances of loss against that of gain, there is no time to hesitate, you must give all. And thus, when one is forced to play, he must renounce reason to preserve his life, rather than risk it for infinite gain, as likely to happen as the loss of nothingness.[2]

Admittedly, Pascal's language is a little difficult to process—it is the language of a philosopher and of probability. More simply, the elements of his bet are as follows:

Premise A: *God may or may not be real.*

Premise B: *If God is real and the Bible is true, then I risk an eternity of life and happiness if I do not serve Him. (More than that I also risk an eternity of infinite misery in hell.)*

Premise C: *If God is not real and I live as if He is, I only lose a finite amount of happiness here on this earth.*

Conclusion: *Therefore, since the infinities of heaven and happiness and of hell and torment outweigh the finiteness of life on earth, I will wager there is a God, and live my life accordingly.*

Let's consider the four possibilities the wager allows for:

Bet 1. If there is a God, and you choose to follow Him, then you will maximize your chance of receiving eternal life, you will make God happy, you will benefit from answered prayers, you will feel God's love in this life, you will be rewarded in the next, and you will be able to help others find salvation.

Bet 2. If there is no God, and you choose to live as if there is a God, then you still get all the benefits of religion, including an ethical system that produces life satisfaction and happiness, and the satisfaction of belonging to a group. However, you do lose the time spent sitting in church, miss out on various types of pleasure, and do not live as free of restraint as you could have.

Bet 3. If there is no God, and you chose to live as if there is no God, then you will not waste time in useless religious ceremonies, you will control your life, and you get to do activities that the Church thinks are sinful with no eternal consequences. In other words, you can drink alcohol, use cuss words, and have sex with whomever you choose and not incur any eternal consequences.

Bet 4. If there is a God, and you choose to live as if there is not a God, then you lose the opportunity to live in heaven for eternity, you make God sad, you fail to live up to the ideals of your Creator, you miss out on the benefits of answered prayer, you miss out on God's love, you will regret how you spent your life here on earth, and you will never find meaning in your life because you are searching in the wrong places.

Four possible outcomes, but only two choices--either believe God exists or do not believe God exists. Thus, if (1) you choose to believe in God and God does in fact exist, you gain infinitely. If (2) you choose to believe in God and He does not exist, your gains and losses are even. If (3) you choose to believe God does not exist and He does not exist, again, your gains and losses are even. If (4) you choose not to believe in God, and God does exist, you lose everything. Based on these alternatives, according to Pascal, it would be foolish for you not to believe in God.

Pascal's bet makes a lot of sense to me. A Christian singer, Marcos Witt, told a secular news anchor, "I choose to bet my life on God's existence. You can bet your life on anything you want to, but I'm betting that God is real, the Bible is true, and there is life after death." Betting on God is the only rational way to bet. Christian Hip Hop artist, Lecrae, observed, "If I'm wrong about God, I wasted my life. If you are wrong about God, you wasted your eternity."

Problems with Pascal's Wager.

Some flaws with Pascal's Wager have been proposed:

1. The Christian God and eternity are not the only options. Pascal's Wager works equally well when applied to Mormonism, Islam, or any other theistic faith. This introduces the problem of which religion should one make a bet on? In examining this problem, Michael Rota concludes, "Practice the religion that seems to you, on careful examination and reflection, most likely to be true."[3] When Christianity is held up against every other religion, it emerges as the most likely to be true.

2. Belief in God could be faked. It has been proposed that Pascal's Wager leaves open the idea that God can be fooled by pretend belief. The solution to this flaw is that God is all-knowing, and therefore He knows if you believe with sincerity or not. However, Christian faith is not merely intellectual, but it practically changes how a person lives. Believing in Jesus includes the choice to love, be kind, be generous, have patience, extend forgiveness, be repentant and much more. To fake belief in God would mean doing all these things, but somehow being fake about them too. Such an experiment would be exhausting to fake believers.

Daring to believe

One of my atheist friends asked me, "How do I choose to believe if I do not believe? The reason I do not believe is not because I don't want to believe, it is because I can't believe." I answered him by saying, "If you feel you cannot believe, ask the God you do not believe in to give you the faith to believe. If you ask, I am confident He will reveal Himself to you."

Jesus once said to a man, "If you can believe, all things are possible to him who believes." The man responded, *"Lord, I believe; help my unbelief"* (Mark 9:24). This man acknowledged that at the same time that he believed, he was also struggling with unbelief. Doubt and problems with belief are not insurmountable problems to God. The key is to not allow your lack of belief or faith to keep you from going to God. There is a proverb that says *"Lean not on your own understanding: In all your ways, acknowledge* [God]*, and He shall direct your paths"* (Proverbs 3:5-6). This means that when we are struggling with unbelief, we have two choices: we can trust our doubts, or we can take that unbelief to God—acknowledging it to Him. If we choose to trust in our unbelief, we will never start believing. But if we take our unbelief to God, He can show us the way to Him.

If you have doubts, or are having difficulty believing, God is on your side. He is not against those who do not believe. As it says in John 3:17: *"God did not send His Son into the world to condemn the world, but that the world through Him might be saved."* The only question that remains is:

Will you DARE to wager that God is real?

PROOF

CHAPTER 17
Making a Choice

Choose for yourselves this day whom you will serve...
But as for me and my house, we will serve the Lord. — Joshua 24:15

As a child, I read *Choose Your Own Adventure* books. If you read them too, you will remember that, at crucial points in the story, the books gave the reader a choice concerning how the hero or heroine will respond. How you choose sends them off on one adventure or another. The same is true in your spiritual walk. God has designed your story so that you have the opportunity to choose your own adventure.

In Deuteronomy 30:19 God explains the choice this way, *"I have set before you life and death, blessing and cursing; therefore choose life."* So, after reading this far, it's up to you as the reader to make a decision. Is God real? Is the Bible true? Is Jesus the Son of God? Do you believe the message of the Bible? Or do you choose not to believe? You get to choose the direction your story takes. But be careful: this decision is bigger than a simple life and death issue (if that could be called simple). Your decision is a question of eternal life and eternal death. Will you choose the way of life that leads to heaven, or will you choose to walk away from God and eventually end up in hell?

The God-shaped hole

There is a great gap, a chasm, between God and humanity. When God created Adam and Eve, He walked and talked with them every day. But, when they sinned, the link between God and man was broken. Because of this there is a God-shaped hole in every human heart. The biblical book of Ecclesiastes refers to this when it says that God *"has set eternity in the human heart"* (Ecclesiastes 3:11). As Saint Augustine wrote in his *Confessions*: "You have made us for yourself, O Lord, and our hearts are restless until they rest in you."

Others throughout history have alluded to the same experience that Augustine writes of. John Calvin, the French Protestant reformer, called this feeling the *"senses divinitatis"* (sense of divinity). He writes,

> *There is within the human mind, and indeed by natural instinct, an awareness of divinity. This we take to be beyond controversy. To prevent anyone from taking refuge in the pretense of ignorance, God Himself has implanted in all men a certain understanding of His divine majesty …Men of sound judgment will alway be sure that a sense of divinity which can never be effaced is engraved upon men's minds. Indeed, the perversity of the impious, who though they struggle furiously are unable to extricate themselves from the fear of God, is abundant testimony that this conviction, namely, that there is some God, is naturally inborn in all, and is fixed deep within, as it were in the very marrow.[1]*

Pascal wrote: "There is a God shaped vacuum in the heart of every person which cannot be filled by any created thing, but only by God, the Creator." He wrote further that:

> *There was once in man a true happiness, of which all that now remains is the empty print and trace. This he tried in vain to fill with everything around him, seeking in things that are not there the help he cannot find in those that are, though none can help, since this infinite abyss can be filled only with an infinite and immutable object, in other words by God Himself.[2]*

C. S. Lewis also wrote about a "God-shaped vacuum" in his book "Screwtape Letters," and Rick Warren, author of *The Purpose Driven Life*, said, "There is a hole in our hearts that only God can fill." The atheist philosopher, Bertrand Russell, (1872-1970) wrote of the hopeless reality of life without God:

> *That man is the product of causes which had no previsions of the end they were achieving; that his origin, his growth, his hopes and fears, his loves and his beliefs, are but the outcome of accidental collocations of atoms; that no fire, no heroism, no intensity of thought and feeling, can preserve an individual life beyond the grave; that all the labors of the ages, all the devotion, all the inspiration, all the noonday brightness of human genius, are destined to extinction in the vast death of the solar system, and that the whole temple of Man's achievement must inevitably be buried under the debris of a universe in ruins—all these things, if not quite beyond dispute, are yet so nearly certain, that no philosophy which rejects them can hope to stand. Only within the scaffolding of these truths, only on the firm foundation of unyielding despair, can the soul's habitation henceforth be safely built.* [3]

Bertrand Russell also wrote that, "The center of me is always and eternally a terrible pain—a curious wild pain—a searching for something beyond what the world contains."

All down the millennia, humans have tried to fill in this hole. Some try to fill it with sex, but after dozens of partners, they find themselves still searching for love. Others think they can fill it with philosophy and intellectualism, but after a lifetime of learning, their doubts persist and they still feel unsatisfied. Others try to fill the hole with pleasure, only to find that fine foods and wines turn to ashes in their mouths. Some seek fame, only to be disappointed with the fleeting glory. Still others seek meaning in sports, but at the end of life, their bodies are broken down and they are unable to compete with younger athletes. Others turn to the highs of drugs and alcohol only to be disappointed by a crash and a hangover the next morning. Sadly, others think that the self-annihilation of suicide is the solution. Others turn to religion to experience a measure of solace.

Atheists often point to the multiplicity of religions as evidence that there is no true religion. But the existence of many different religions only proves how truly there is a hole inside humans that continually seeks God. We can deny the feeling, run away from it, try to ignore it—but there it is. When we are hungry, there is a feeling in the pit of our stomachs that prompts us to seek food. In the same way, the hole in our souls makes us hungry for our Creator. As C.S. Lewis wrote:

> Creatures are not born with desires unless satisfaction for those desires exists. A baby feels hunger; well, there is such a thing as food. A duckling wants to swim; well, there is such a thing as water. Men feel sexual desire; well there is such a thing as sex. If I find in myself a desire which no experience in this world can satisfy, the most probable explanation is that I was made for another world. If none of my earthly desires satisfy it, that does not prove that the universe is a fraud. Probably earthly desires were never meant to satisfy it, but only to arouse it, to suggest the real thing.[4]

Humans desire purpose and meaning. So, there must be a means for this desire to be fulfilled. Humans have an innate sense of the divine. So, there must be a Divinity to satisfy it. Humans have a God-shaped hole inside them, so there must be a God who can fill it.

The loggerhead sea turtle returns to lay its eggs on the same beach where it was born. The turtle travels thousands of miles in the oceans of the world, but it always finds its way home using an internal GPS system that uses the Earth's magnetic field.[5] In a similar way, each human has an internal GPS system that points towards heaven.

This difference between what we experience in life and what we believe we should be experiencing is the real "missing link" in human history. Jesus Christ came from heaven to earth to restore that link and create a new way for God and humanity to be connected once again. When Jesus died on the cross and rose from the dead, He became the bridge between God and people, between heaven and earth. He is the only way to God, the only way to heaven. As He said: *"I am the way, the truth, and the life. No one comes to the Father except through Me"* (John 14:6).

Understanding the gap

As mentioned earlier in the chapter, sin is what opened the gap between people and God. Adam and Eve chose an adventure for themselves and humanity: sin. The consequences of their choice have affected humanity ever since. The problem with sin is that it always has consequences. The Bible says, *"Be sure your sin will find you out"* (Numbers 32:23). Later, it warns, *"The wages of sin is death"* (Romans 6:23). For some people the consequences of sin catch up immediately, and for others it takes longer for the price to be revealed. But ultimately, sin will take you farther than you want to go, keep you longer than you want to stay, and cost you more than you want to pay.

This problem of sin is universal. The Bible says, *"All have sinned and fallen short of the glory of God"* (Romans 3:23). Earlier in the same chapter the Apostle Paul tells us, *"There is none righteous, no, not one"* (Romans 3:10). Every person has made mistakes and fallen short of his or her own standards of what is good and right, let alone God's standards. Look around at our world: crime, racism, bigotry, hate, and war continue to increase despite humanity's best efforts to overcome them.

For a time, there was optimism that science held the answers that humanity is seeking. The Enlightenment exalted human reason and hoped that human wisdom would lead to peace and happiness for the whole world. This hope was brutally shattered by World War I and II and the subsequent Cold War between the United States and the Communist World. The same science that promised to cure disease also taught us how to kill more efficiently. Philosophies that promised hope for those trapped in poverty ended up enslaving and murdering millions of people. Our best efforts have not solved the problem of evil.

Part of the reason is that humanity has to go beyond asking, "Why is there evil in the world?" to asking, "Why is there evil in me?" Despite my best efforts, why do I mess up sometimes? I want to love my wife, but sometimes I lose my temper. I want to obey the law, but sometimes I get a speeding ticket. Why is it so hard to do what is right? I know the difference between right and wrong, but sometimes my own selfishness, lust, and pride compel me to act in ways that are detrimental to my long-term happiness. The Russian novelist Aleksandr Solzhenitsyn (1918-2008) wrote, "the line separating good and evil passes not through states, nor between classes, nor between political parties either, but right through every human heart." The problem of evil is addressed not by trying to fix evil, but by addressing the problem of sin.

Addressing the problem of sin can be tricky. Sin is deceptive—like the weavers in the fairy tale who convince the emperor that only hopelessly stupid people won't admire the wonderful clothes they have dressed him in. The emperor, not wanting to be hopelessly stupid, and his court, wanting to maintain favor with the emperor, admire the work of the weavers. The only problem is, the weavers haven't woven any clothes, and the emperor is walking around naked. Only when a child blurts out the truth, does everyone begin to acknowledge the problem. In the same way, sin blinds people to the problem of sin. One reason discussing apologetics with non-believers is so difficult is because sin keeps them from seeing God or acknowledging their need of Him. The only way to remove this blindfold of sin is to put one's faith in God's child, Jesus Christ.

Jesus paid the price to redeem us from sin

The only way to fill the hole in your heart is to meet the Creator your heart longs for. Right now, that hole is filled with sin. It might be filled with lust, pride, addiction, hate, fear, or pain. The only thing that can remove the sin and fill the hole is a relationship with Jesus Christ. Once you meet Jesus, He will fill your heart and your sin will disappear.

This is the miracle of Christianity. God became a man and came to earth to live here among His creations. Jesus, the Son of God, was born to the Virgin Mary and walked the dusty streets of Israel. He lived a perfect life and then He gave His life on the cross to pay the price for the sins of humanity. We deserve to die because of our sins, but Christ died in our place. Jesus' death paid the price for our sins and His resurrection proves that God accepted His death as payment for our sins. As the Bible says, *"But God demonstrates His own love toward us, in that while we were still sinners, Christ died for us"* (Romans 5:8). This is good news because it means we can be saved from our sins. We can choose a new adventure. The Bible says, *"If you confess with your mouth the Lord Jesus and believe in your heart that God has raised Him from the dead, you will be saved"* (Romans 10:9).

I know of an old man in Africa. Once, he was walking down a road and carrying a heavy sack of rice. He had recently been saved and he was telling everyone he knew about what had happened when Jesus came into his life. On his way, he met an educated foreigner who was an atheist. The unbeliever said to the old man, "How can you know you are saved? Nobody can ever really know such a thing." The man threw down the sack of rice and replied, "How do I know I'm not carrying the bag of rice? I'm not looking at it." The atheist said, "You feel less weight on your back." The old man explained, "That's exactly how I know I'm saved. I no longer feel the heavy burden of my sin."

What happens when you choose to follow Jesus?

1. You are saved from sin. God's Word promises, *"Everyone who calls on the name of the Lord shall be saved"* (Romans 10:13). The problem of evil in the world will in a measure be solved because you are choosing to let God deal with the problem of sin in you. As Romans 8:1 says, *"There is therefore now no condemnation to those who are in Christ Jesus, who do not walk according to the flesh, but according to the Spirit."*

2. You will have peace with God. *"Therefore, having been justified by faith, we have peace with God through our Lord Jesus Christ…"* (Romans 5:1). This means that the missing link, the gaping hole, will finally be filled. Instead of an ache in the center of your being, instead of feeling lost, or adrift, or purposeless, you will have peace, and, in Jesus you will have a friend to take all your worries to.

3. You become a new person. The Apostle Paul says: *"If anyone is in Christ, he is a new creation; old things have passed away; behold, all things have become new"* (2 Corinthians 5:17). You may have been born a sinner, but when you put your faith in Jesus, you are "born again" as a saint and a child of God. This doesn't mean that you are perfect, or that you can judge others, it means that you are free to choose God's adventure for you.

4. You can be sure that you will go to heaven. Heaven is the eternal home of God's people. No matter the problems that evil can bring into this world or your life, it can never change God's love for you or separate you from Him. As the Apostle Paul wrote, *"For I am persuaded that neither death nor life, nor angels nor principalities nor powers, nor things present nor things to come, nor height nor depth, nor any other created thing, shall be able to separate us from the love of God which is in Christ Jesus our Lord"* (Romans 8:38-39).

Will you DARE?

The life of an atheist is sad because it is going nowhere. Once there was an atheist who died and was buried. On his tombstone was written, "Here lies an atheist—all dressed up and no place to go." When atheist Christopher Hitchens died, I tweeted, "Either Hitchens knows that he was wrong, or he does not know that he was right." Of course, I was attacked viciously by the atheist Twitter community.

In some ways I have great respect for atheists. They believe strongly in evidence. They are skeptical. They reject non-scientific mumbo jumbo and the claims of pseudo-science. They reject superstition. They are willing to change their minds as evidence changes. Even if they have not found the right answers, at least they are asking life's big questions.

At the same time, I deeply pity atheists. They value evidence above all else, but they cannot see the overwhelming evidence for God's existence. It is intellectually dishonest to deny God's existence since all creation shouts, "God is THERE!" As G. K. Chesterton wrote in one of his Father Brown mysteries: "What we all dread most," said the priest, in a low voice, "Is a maze with no center. That is why atheism is only a nightmare."[6] Others have echoed Chesterton. Daniel Kolenda wrote, "The devil loves atheists, although he is not one himself." Or as the Usual Suspects movie puts it, "The greatest trick the devil ever pulled was convincing the world he didn't exist."

But there is hope, even for the hardcore atheist. Perhaps the patron saint of the atheist is "doubting" Thomas. He demanded verifiable proof of Jesus' resurrection:

> *Now Thomas…one of the twelve, was not with them when Jesus came. The other disciples therefore said to him, "We have seen the Lord. So he said to them, "Unless I see in His hands the print of the nails, and put my finger into the print of the nails, and put my hand into His side, I will not believe." And after eight days His disciples were again inside, and Thomas with them. Jesus came, the doors being shut, and stood in the midst, and said, "Peace to you!" Then He said to Thomas, "Reach your finger here, and look at My hands; and reach your hand here, and put it into My side. Do not be unbelieving, but believing." And Thomas answered and said to Him, "My Lord and my God!" Jesus said to him, "Thomas, because you have seen Me, you have believed. Blessed are those who have not seen and yet have believed."* (John 20:24-29)

Jesus offers Thomas the chance to test the resurrection with his own finger, but Jesus says it is better to believe without proof. In the same way, God is willing to offer proof to the atheist who sincerely searches for it, but those who believe without seeing will be even more blessed.

True wisdom for life begins with the acknowledgment of God's existence. *"The fear of the Lord is the beginning of knowledge: but fools despise wisdom and instruction"* (Proverbs 1:7). Ultimately, God is discovered by those who look for Him. As Jesus said to the two blind men who were seeking healing, *"According to your faith be it done onto you"* (Matthew 9:29). Your faith determines whether you ever see God.

There is an old saying: "Don't put off till tomorrow what you can do today." The Bible says, *"Now is the day of salvation"* (2 Corinthians 6:2), and that *"Today, if you will hear His voice"* (Hebrews 3:7), you can be saved. Whatever you have been believing about God, today is a day for faith, today is a day to be daring. You've read some of the evidence. You've examined some of the proof. Today you can choose to believe that God exists, that God created you, that God loves you, and that God is as close as a simple prayer.

Perhaps you are tempted to put off deciding. That's not how it works. You must choose your own adventure. To not choose is just to keep choosing the story you've been telling yourself, or the one that you believe because others have told you it must be true. The Bible promises that eventually, every knee will bow and every tongue will confess that Jesus is Lord (Romans 14:11 and Philippians 2.10-11). No matter how you choose today, someday everyone will be presented with irrefutable proof of God's existence when he or she stands in front of the throne of God Almighty. But, by then it will be too late to choose, too late to dare, for that is the end of your story.

But, today is not too late. Your adventure waits. Call on Jesus, the Son of God, and He will save you and set your story on a whole new course. God is THERE. God does CARE. Will you DARE to choose to follow Him? If so, pray this simple prayer. The prayer itself will not save you, it is by putting your faith in Jesus Christ that you will be saved. Repeating this prayer is a way for you to tell God that you are daring to believe in Him and are ready to trust in Jesus Christ for your salvation:

If you dare to trust God for salvation, pray this prayer:

Dear God in heaven,

I believe You exist, and I need You in my life. Thank you for caring for me. I believe that Jesus is the Son of God, that He died on a cross for my sins, and that He rose from the dead. Today, I dare to put my faith and trust in Him. Jesus, I make You the Lord of my life, and I repent of my unbelief and all the things I have done wrong. Please forgive me and give me a brand-new start.

In the Name of Jesus I pray,

Amen.

If you have decided to follow Jesus today, send me an e-mail:

daniel@kingministries.com

and I will send you an e-copy of my book: *Welcome to the Kingdom* to help you with the next steps of your walk with God.

FOOTNOTES

Foreword

[1] Jim Burkett, "The Imperative of Apologetics: Evidence-Based Evangelism and Transforming Culture," Unpublished article.

[2] John R. W. Stott, *Your Mind Matters* (Downers Grove, IL: InterVarsity Press, 1972), 13.

Introduction

[1] Ravi Zacharias, "Think Again—Deep Questions," https://www.rzim.org/read/just-thinking-magazine/think-again-deep-questions (October 1, 2019).

[1] Illustration from J.P. Moreland

[2] Isaac Newton, *Principia*

[3] Thomas Aquinas, *Summa Theologica*

[4] William Lane Craig, *On Guard* (Colorado Springs, CO: David C. Cook, 2010), 100.

[1] William Paley, *Natural Theology* (Boston, MA: Richardson, Lord & Holbrook, and Crocker & Brewster, 1831), 9-10.

[2] Serge Brunier, *Majestic Universe: Views from Here to Infinity* (Cambridge: Cambridge University Press, 1999), 93.

[3] Plato, *Laws* 12.966e.

[4] Aristotle, *On Philosophy*.

[5] Cicero, *De Natura Deorum*.

[6] Norman Geisler, *The Big Book of Christian Apologetics*, (Grand Rapids, MI: Baker Books, 2012), 22.

[7] Geisler, 22.

[8] Geisler, 22.

[9] Geisler, 22.

[10] Geisler, 22.

[11] Geisler, 22.

[12] Richard Dawkins, *The God Delusion* (New York, NY: Houghton Mifflin Company, 2006), 137.

[13] William Lane Craig, *On Guard* (Colorado Springs, CO: David C. Cook, 2010), 116.

[14] Charles Darwin, *Origin of Species* (1872), 6th ed. (New York: New York University Press, 1988), 154.

[15] Stephen C. Meyer, *Signature in the Cell*, (New York, NY: Harper One, 2009).

[16] Dawkins, *The God Delusion*, 137-138.

[17] Scott Hahan and Benjamin Wiker, *Answering the New Atheism* (Stenbenville, OH: Emmaus Road Publishing, 2008), 27.

[18] Richard Dawkins, *The Blind Watchmaker* (New York, NY: W.W. Norton & Company, 1987) 161.

[19] Michael Behe, *Darwin's Black Box: The Biochemical Challenge to Evolution* (New York: Free Press, 2006), 70.

3. Ontological Proof–The Evidence from Abstract Reasoning.........33

[1] John M. Frame, *Apologetics to the Glory of God* (Phillipsburg, NJ: P&R Publishing, 1994), 115.

[2] Critics of the ontological proof include Thomas Aquinas, David Hume, and Immanuel Kant.

[3] Alvin Plantinga, *God, Freedom, and Evil* (Grand Rapids, MI: William B. Eerdmans Publishing, 1974), 83-112.

[4] Douglas Groothuis, *Christian Apologetics* (Downers Grove, IL: InterVarsity, 2011), 199-200.

4. Morality Proof–The Evidence from Right and Wrong 39

[1] Kant, *Critique of Practical Reason.*

[2] C.S. Lewis, *Mere Christianity* (New York: MacMillan, 1952), 21.

[3] Greg M. Epstein, *Good Without God* (New York, NY: HarperCollins, 2009), 34. Epstein says the ethics of a humanist come from human needs and interests tested by experience.

[4] Paul Little, *Know Why You Believe* (Downers Grove, IL: InterVarsity Press, 2008), 24.

[5] Fyodor Dostoevsky, *The Brothers Karamazov,* (London: Encyclopedia Britannica, 1952), 312.

[6] Dostoevsky, 314.

5. Scripture Proof–Evidence from the Bible............................... 49

[1] John Rylands Papyri, P. 52, *A.D.* 125.

[2] Norman Geisler, "A Note on the Percent of Accuracy of the New Testament Text," https://normangeisler.com/a-note-on-the-percent-of-accuracy-of-the-new-testament-text/, (August 3, 2020).

[3] Sir William M Ramsey, *The Bearing of Recent Discovery on the Trustworthiness of the New Testament* (London; New York; Toronto: Hodder & Stoughton, 1915), 222.

[4] Norman Geisler, *Baker Encyclopedia of Apologetics* (Grand Rapids: Baker Books, 1999), 47.

[5] For the above and further historical evidence, see Bible and Archaeology—Online Museum, http://bibleandarchaeology.com, (June 25, 2020).

[6] Mark Spence, "Can We Trust the Bible?" https://www. livingwaters.com/can-we-trust-the-bible. (June 25, 2020).

6. Scripture Proof 2–More Evidence from the Bible 63

[1] Dan Delzell, "Does Christianity Stand on Faith or Evidence?" *The Christian Post*, October 23, 2011, http://www.christianpost.com/news/does-christianity-stand-on-faith-or-evidence-59046, (May 4, 2020).

7. Supernatural Proof–Evidence from Miracles 79

[1] Princeton Survey Research Associates, Newsweek poll, April 13-14, 2000.

[2] David Hume, The Philosophical Works of David Hume, Vol. 4. "Of Miracles", (Edinburgh, Adam Black and William Tair and Charles Tait, 1826), 130.

[3] David Hume, 141.

[4] Craig Keener, *Miracles: The Credibility of the New Testament Accounts,* 2 vols. (Grand Rapids, MI: Baker Academic, 2011).

8. Redemptive Proof–Evidence from Religious Experience 91

[1] Attributed to Stephen F. Roberts.

² Luis Palau, *God is Relevant* (New York, NY: Doubleday, 1997), 81.

³ William Lane Craig, "The Problem of Miracles: A Historical and Philosophical Perspective," Reasonable Faith with William Lane Craig, https://www.reasonablefaith.org/writings/scholarly-writings/historical-jesus/the-problem-of-miracles-a-historical-and-philosophical-perspective, (June 25, 2020).

⁴ Blaise Pascal, *Pensées,* 3.242, in *Great Books of the Western World* (London, Encyclopedia Britannica, 1952), 218.

Part 2: Does God CARE?

¹ The OmniPoll, conducted by Barna Research Group, Ltd., January 1999. Quoted in Lee Strobel, *The Case for Faith: A Journalist Investigates the Toughest Objections to Christianity.* (Grand Rapids, MI: Zondervan, 2000), 29.

² H. J. McCloskey, "God and Evil," *Philosophical Quarterly* (1960): 10: 97-114.

³ Harold S. Kushner, *When Bad Things Happen to Good People* (New York: Schocken Books, 1981).

⁴ Alan Carter, "On Pascal's Wager: Or All Bets are Off?" *Philosophia Christi,* 2nd ser., 3, no. 2 (2001): 511-16.

⁵ Alvin Plantinga, *God, Freedom, and Evil* (Grand Rapids, MI: William B. Eerdmans Publishing, 1974), 30.

⁶ C. S. Lewis, *Mere Christianity* (New York, NY: Macmillan, 1943), 52.

⁷ C. S. Lewis, *Mere Christianity,* 45.

⁸ Dorothy L. Sayers, *Letters to a Diminished Church: Passionate Arguments for the Relevance of Christian Doctrine*

[1] C.S. Lewis, *Miracles* (New York, NY: Touchstone, 1996), 143.

[1] Lee Strobal, *The Case for Christ* (Grand Rapids, MI: Zondervan, 1998).

[2] David Limbaugh, "Contradictions in the Gospels," Real Clear Religion, http://www.realclearreligion.org/articles/2017/04/12/contradictions_in_the_gospels_110125.html (June 25, 2020).

[3] Flavius Josephus, *Antiquities of the Jews* 20.9.1

[4] Josephus, 18.63-64, 18.63f, 18.3.3

[5] Pliny, *Epistles* 10.96

[6] Tacitus, *Annals* 15.44

[7] Suetonius, *The Lives of the Twelve Caesars*, Claudius 25.

[8] *The Babylonian Talmud,* transl. by I. Epstein (London: Soncino, 1935), vol. III, Sanhedrin 43a, 281

[9] Lucian, "The Death of Peregrine," 11-13, in *The Works of Lucian of Samosata,* transl. by H.W. Fowler and F.G. Fowler, 4 vols. (Oxford: Clarendon, 1949), vol. 4.

[1] C. S. Lewis, *Mere Christianity* (New York, NY: Macmillan, 1943), 56.

[2] Mahatma Gandhi, "What Jesus Means to Me," *The Modern Review* (October 1941), republished on mahatma.org.in

[1] Gary Habermas, *The Historical Jesus* (Joplin, MO: College Press, 1996), 158.

[2] Craig A. Evens and N.T. Wright, *Jesus, the Final Days* (Louisville, KY: Westminister John Knox Press, 2009), 105.

[1] Thomas Aquinas, *Summa Theologica,* 1.1.6.2.

[2] Sam Harris, *Letter to a Christian Nation* (New York: Knopf, 2007), 63.

[3] Christopher Hitchens, *God is Not Great: How Religion Poisons Everything* (New York: Hachette Books, 2007), 55

[4] Richard Dawkins, *The God Delusion* (New York, NY: Mariner, 2008), 321.

[5] Carl Sagan, *The Demon-Haunted World: Science as a Candle in the Dark* (New York: Random House. 1995), 12.

[6] Ravi Zacharias, *The End of Reason* (Grand Rapids, MI: Zondervan, 2008), 117.

[7] Jeremy Wallace, "Misc. Theistic Arguments," July 7, 2018, https://vimeo.com/278858983, (August 3, 2020).

[1] Peter Boghossian, *A Manual for Creating Atheists* (Durham, NC: Pitchstone Publishing, 2013), 1.

[2] A lecture by Richard Dawkins extracted from The Nullifidian (December 1994), http://www.simonyi.ox.ac.uk/dawkins/

WorldOfDawkins-archive/Dawkins/Work/ Articles/1994-12religion.shtml, (August 3, 2020).

[3] Mark Twain, *Following the Equator* (New York: Dover, 1989), 132.

[4] Ravi Zacharias, *Jesus Among Other Gods* (Nashville, TN: Thomas Nelson, 2000), 58.

[5] Augustine, *Tractates on the Gospel of John,* trans. John W. Rettig (Washington, D.C.: Catholic University of American Press, 1988), 29.6.2.

[6] Anselm, *Proslogion,* trans. S. N. Deane, 2nd ed. (Chicago: Open Court, 1962), chap. 1.

[7] Robert G. Tuttle, *The Story of Evangelism* (Nashville, TN: Abingdon, 2006), 206.

[8] John Locke, *An Essay Concerning Human Understanding* (1690).

[9] Blaise Pascal, *Pensées* 4.277-278, in *Great Books of the Western World* (London, Encyclopedia Britannica, 1952), 222.

[10] Jeremy Wallace, "Misc. Theistic Arguments," (July 7, 2018) https://vimeo.com/278858983#at=795, (August 3, 2020).

[11] See Soren Kierkegarrd, *Concluding Unscientific Postscript to Philosophical Fragments,* ed. Howard Hong and Edna Hong, (Princeton, NJ: Princeton University, 1992). *(Page 161)*

16. High Stakes Choices

[1] Blaise Pascal, *The Mind on Fire,* James Houston, ed. (Colorado Springs, CO: Victor Books, 2006), 43.

[2] Blaise Pascal, *Pensées* 3.233, in *Great Books of the Western World* (London, Encyclopedia Britannica, 1952), 214-115.

[3] Michael Rota, *Taking Pascal's Wager* (Downer's Grove, IL: Intervarsity, 2016), 67.

17. Making a Choice

[1] John Calvin, *Institutes of the Christian Religion* (Philadelphia: Westminster Press, 1960), 43, 45-46.

[2] Blaise Pascal, *Pensees* 133/169, ed. and trans. Alban Krailsheimer (New York: Penguin, 1966), 75.

[3] Bertrand Russell, "A Free Man's Worship," *Mysticism and Logic and Other Essays* (BiblioLife; General Books, 2010), 47-48 Quoted in True Reason (87).

[4] C. S. Lewis, *Mere Christianity* (New York, NY: Macmillan, 1943), 120.

[5] Carrie Arnold, "How Do Sea Turtles Find the Exact Beach Where They Were Born?" National Geographic (January 16, 2015), http://news.nationalgeographic.com/news/2015/01/150115-loggerheads-sea-turtles-navigation-magnetic-field-science/. (June 25, 2020).

[6] C. K. Chesterton, *The Father Brown Omnibus,* 319.

Suggested Reading & Resources

Apologetics

Beckwith, Francis J. and William Lane Craig, J.P. Moreland, eds. *To Everyone An Answer: A Case for the Christian Worldview.* Downers Grove, IL: IVP Books, 2004.

Baucham Jr., Voddie. *Expository Apologetics.* Wheaton, IL: Crossway, 2015.

Boa, Kenneth D., and Robert M. Bowman. *20 Compelling Evidences that God Exists.* Tulsa, OK: RiverOak, 2002.

Chesterton, G.K. *Heretics / Orthodoxy.* Nashville, TN: Thomas Nelson, 2000.

Craig, William Lane. *On Guard.* Colorado Springs, CO: David C. Cook, 2010.

Craig, William Lane. *Reasonable Faith.* Wheaton, IL: Crossway Books, 2008.

Craig, William Lane and Walter Sinnott-Armstrong. *God? A Debate Between a Christian and an Atheist.* New York, NY: Oxford University Press, 2004.

DeWeese, Garrett J. *Doing Philosophy as a Christian.* Downers Grove, IL: Intervarsity Press, 2011.

Dyrness, William. *Christian Apologetics in a World Community.* Downers Grove, IL: IVP Books, 1983.

Dulles, Avery Cardinal. *A History of Apologetics.* Eugene, Oregon: Wipf and Stock, 1999.

Evens, Craig A., and N.T. Wright. *Jesus, the Final Days.* Louisville, KY: Westminster John Knox Press, 2009.

Evens, Craig A., *Fabricating Jesus: How Modern Scholars Distort the Gospel.* Downers Grove, IL: IVP Books, 2006.

Evens, Craig A., and Emanuel Tov, eds. *Exploring the Origins of the Bible.* Grand Rapids, MI: Baker Academic, 2008.

Feser, Edward. *Five Proofs of the Existence of God.* San Francisco, CA: Ignatius Press, 2017.

Frame, John M. *Apologetics to the Glory of God.* Phillipsburg, NJ: P&R Publishing, 1994.

Geisler, Norman L. *The Big Book of Christian Apologetics.* Grand Rapids, MI: Baker Books, 2012.

Geisler, Norman L., and Frank Turek. *I Don't Have Enough Faith to Be an Atheist.* Wheaton, IL: Crossway, 2004.

Gilson, Tom, and Carso Weitnauer, eds. *True Reason: Christian Responses to the Challenge of Atheism.* Englewood, CA: Patheos Press, 2012.

Groothuis, Douglas. *Christian Apologetics.* Downers Grove, IL: InterVarsity, 2011.

Hahn, Scott, and Benjamin Wiker. *Answering the New Atheism.* Steubenville, OH: Emmaus Road Publishing, 2008.

House, H. Wayne, and Dennis W. Jowers, *Reasons for Our Hope: An Introduction to Christian Apologetics,* Nashville, TN: B&H, 2011.

Jeffrey, Grant R. *Jesus, the Great Debate.* Toronto, Ontario: Frontier Research, 1999.

Keller, Timothy. *The Reason for God*. New York, NY: Riverhead Books, 2008.

Koukl, Gregory. *Tactics*. Grand Rapids, MI: Zondervan, 2009.

Lennox, John C. *Gunning for God: Why the New Atheists are Missing the Target*. Oxford, England: Lion Books, 2011.

Lewis, C.S. *The Case for Christianity*. New York, NY: Macmillan, 1944.

Lewis, C.S. *Miracles*. New York, NY: Touchstone, 1996.

Little, Paul E. *Know Why You Believe*. Downer's Grove, IL: IVP Books, 2008.

Limbaugh, David. *The Emmaus Code*. Washington, DC: Regnery Publishing, 2015.

McDowell, Josh. *The New Evidence that Demands a Verdict*. Nashville, TN: Thomas Nelson, 1999.

McDowell, Josh. Complied by Bill Wilson. *A Ready Defense*. Nashville, TN: Thomas Nelson, 1993.

Morley, Brian K. *Mapping Apologetics*. Downer's Grove, IL: Intervarsity Press, 2015.

Morris, Thomas V. *Francis Schaeffer's Apologetics: A Critique*. Grand Rapids, MI: Baker Book House, 1987.

Plantinga, Alvin. *God, Freedom, and Evil*. Grand Rapids, MI: William B. Eerdmans Publishing, 1974.

Plantinga, Alvin. *The Nature of Necessary.* Oxford: Oxford University Press. 1974.

Rota, Michael. *Taking Pascal's Wager.* Downer's Grove, IL: Intervarsity, 2016.

Pendedgrass, David W. *A Skeptic Challenges a Christian.* Houston, TX: Perspicacious, 2011.

Schaeffer, Francis. *The God Who Is There.* Downer's Grove, Intervarsity Press, 1968.

Schaeffer, Francis. *How Should We Then Live?* Old Tappan, NJ: Fleming H. Revell, 1976.

Sire, James W. *The Universe Next Door.* Downers Grove, IL: IVP Academic, 2009.

Sproul, R.C., John Gerstner, Arthur Lindsley, *Classical Apologetics.* Grand Rapids, MI: Academie Books, 1984.

Sproul, R.C. *Defending Your Faith.* Wheaton, IL: Crossway, 2003.

Story, Dan. *Defending Your Faith.* Nashville, TN: Thomas Nelson, 1992.

Strobel, Lee. *The Case for Christ.* Grand Rapids, MI: Zondervan, 1998.

Strobel, Lee. *The Case for Faith: A Journalist Investigates the Toughest Objections to Christianity.* Grand Rapids, MI: Zondervan, 2000.

Strobel, Lee. *The Case for a Creator.* Grand Rapids, MI: Zondervan, 2004.

Turek, Frank. *Stealing from God.* Colorado Springs, CO: Nav Press, 2014.

Van Til, Cornelius. *Christian Apologetics.* Phillipsburg, NJ: P&R Publishing, 2003.

Wallace, J. Warner. *Cold Case Christianity.* Colorado Springs, CO: David C. Cook, 2013.

Wright, N.T. *The Resurrection of the Son of God.* Minneapolis, MN: Fortress Press, 2003.

Zacharias, Ravi. *The End of Reason: A Response to the New Atheists.* Grand Rapids, MI: Zondervan, 2008.

Science and Evolution

Behe, Michael. *Darwin's Black Box: The Biochemical Challenge to Evolution.* New York: Free Press, 2006.

Meyer, Stephen C. *Signature in the Cell.* New York, NY: Harper One, 2009.

Miller, Kenneth R. *Finding Darwin's God.* New York, NY: Cliff Street Books, 1999.

ABOUT THE AUTHOR

D r. Daniel King is a missionary evangelist who has traveled to over seventy nations in his quest for souls. His goal is to lead 1,000,000 people to Jesus every year through massive Gospel Festivals, distribution of literature, and leadership training.

Because of his experience and research on evangelism, he is widely regarded as one of the world's leading experts in mass evangelism. He has spoken to more than 2,000 live audiences around the world with attendance of up to 50,000 people and has led over two million individuals in a salvation prayer.

Daniel is the host of *The Evangelism Podcast*, a popular program known for sharing powerful stories about what God is doing around the world, for training evangelists and everyday believers to share their faith, and for exploring the best methods for church growth. He is often called "The Evangelism Coach" because of his passion for training other evangelists.

Daniel graduated *summa cum laude* from Oral Roberts University in 2002 with a B.A. degree in New Testament Studies, with a Master of Divinity degree in 2014, and with a Doctorate of Ministry degree in 2019. The focus of his doctoral research was mass evangelism.

He was called into the ministry when he was five years old and began to preach when he was six. His parents became missionaries to Mexico when he was ten. Daniel spent the next thirteen years ministering in Mexico alongside his parents. When he was fourteen he started a children's ministry that gave him the opportunity to minister in some of America's largest churches while he was still a teenager. Daniel recently celebrated twenty years of full-time ministry.

He is the author of over twenty books including *The Secret of Obed-Edom, Healing Power, Fire Power, Soul Winning, and Grace Wins*. Over 600,000 of his books are in print.

He is married to Jessica. They have two children, Caleb and Katie Grace and they live in Tulsa, Oklahoma, USA.

Daniel is available to speak at your church or conference on apologetics or evangelism.

To invite him to your event or for evangelism coaching, please visit:

www.KingMinistries.com

The vision of King Ministries
is to lead 1,000,000 people to Jesus every year
and to train believers to become leaders.

To contact Daniel & Jessica King:

Write:
King Ministries International
PO Box 701113
Tulsa, OK 74170 USA

King Ministries Canada
PO Box 3401
Morinville, Alberta T8R 1S3 Canada

Call toll-free:
1-877-431-4276

Visit us online:
www.KingMinistries.com

E-Mail:
daniel@kingministries.com

Made in United States
Orlando, FL
26 June 2023

34533612R00115